Amazon Heart

Coping With Breast Cancer
Warrior Princess Style

by
Megan Dwyer and Meredith Campbell

AMAZON HEART –
COPING WITH BREAST CANCER
WARRIOR PRINCESS STYLE

Published by
Artemisia Enterprises, LLC
San Jose, California

Copyright © 2004 by Artemisia Enterprises
Cover Image © Artemisia Enterprises, LLC

Book and Cover Design by Layne Moore
Amazon Heart Logo Design by Carlosus Creative

Library of Congress Control Number
2004094428

ISBN 0-9755416-0-9
www.artemisiaenterprises.com
www.amazon-heart.com

Printed in the United States of America

Dedication

For John, Always
-- Meredith

and

For Madison, Iman and Ibrahim
-- Megan

Acknowledgements

This book, and our journeys, would not have been possible without the support of so many people. I would like to thank John and Dexter for their support and love not only through writing this book, but through my life and my journey with breast cancer. I'd also like to thank my family and friends for their support over the last couple of years through my treatment and beyond, particularly my sister Suzanne who walked with me through every day of my experience with breast cancer, and whose professional input and guidance was invaluable in creating this book and our future projects. - MC

Thank you Mom and Shannon for your endless support always. Thank you Iman for always bringing joy and perspective to my life when I am stuck. And thank you to all of the many friends and family members who have contributed to me in so many ways. I am incredibly touched by your generosity and immensely grateful for your love and support. - MD

Disclaimer

"I really had a flash of vulnerability after my surgery. I felt like my heart was totally exposed. My protective layer was gone and my heart was right there at the surface."

MEGAN DWYER

The Amazon warriors of Greek legend were renowned as strong and independent fighters, famed for removing one breast to improve the accuracy of their archers. The title, Amazon Heart, reflects the challenge we both faced in incorporating the emotional vulnerability and fragility brought by a diagnosis of cancer, with our strong and independent natures.

Thank you for sharing our journeys.

Megan Dwyer and Meredith Campbell

Table of Contents

Timeline

September 2000	Meredith's Diagnosis
July 2001	Meredith completes treatment
August 2001	Meredith's trip to India
June 2002	Megan's Diagnosis
July 2002	Megan's trip to Montana
September 2002	Megan completes treatment
November 2002	Megan and Meredith meet
February 2003	Idea for this book created
June 2003	Megan and Meredith's fundraising walk in San Francisco

Key Players

Some names have been changed to protect individuals' privacy.

Sharon and Elliot	Megan's life partner and her dog
Shannon and Iman	Megan's sister and Shannon's daughter
John and Dexter	Meredith's husband and her son
Suzanne	Meredith's sister
Julie and Jules	Meredith's sister and Julie's life partner

Part I:

What's it all About?

When Megan Met Meredith

Each friend represents a world in us,
a world possibly not born until they arrive,
and it is only by this meeting that a new world is born.

ANAIS NIN

As I go through life, I recognize more and more that everything happens for a reason, although it is sometimes hard to figure out at the time what the reason could possibly be.

In September of 2000, my life partner Sharon and I started taking sailing lessons in San Francisco. We'd never really sailed before, but we had dreams of chartering a boat and sailing the Greek Isles. I had no idea at the time where that decision to learn to sail would take me.

Five days later, halfway around the world, Meredith had just been diagnosed with breast cancer. She was a healthy, active 33 year old, lifelong sailor living in Brisbane, Australia with her husband and son.

It seems to me, looking back on events, that we were destined to meet. Destined to meet and become friends and create this book. But that all happened two years later.

Through the course of our sailing lessons, Sharon and I learned of the Gay Games (an inclusive sporting and cultural event modeled after the Olympics, open to all). The next one was in November of 2002, in Sydney, Australia, and sailing was one of the events. We decided we had to go and participate, so our sailing efforts shifted from cruising to racing.

In June, 2002, almost two years after we started our sailing lessons, I too was diagnosed with breast cancer as a healthy, active 35 year old. Meredith had finished her treatment one year earlier, and was now considering her own Gay Games appearance as Captain of the Three Cheese Fagottinis.

I was determined to get to Australia that year, and influenced the timing of my treatment as much as I could to ensure I could not only go, but actually compete. Five weeks after my last chemo treatment, my sailing team took silver medals in Sydney Harbour as competitors in the Gay Games. Meredith was there too, captaining her team to a double gold medal performance.

In retrospect, it is amazing how close we came to not meeting at all. It was day 5 of a 6 day regatta. It had been an especially terrifying, windy, challenging day on the water, and many of the sailors were enjoying a post-sail recovery drink in the yacht club. OK, it was all of the Australian sailors plus Sharon and me.

As "luck" would have it, Meredith and I were sitting next to each other. We probably still would not have talked to each other left to our own introverted ways, so the Universe stepped in to give us a nudge.

Sharon mentioned that I had just finished treatment for breast cancer, and Meredith turned and gave me a high five. I was totally stunned to meet someone so cool who had been through it too.

The connection and bond between us was immediate. It helped that we were able to laugh about our experiences, that we had similar interests and were the same age. And there was something even deeper than all of that. We both really connected with each other in an instant.

The next day, Meredith gave me her team uniform from the opening ceremonies and I gave her my Team San Francisco jacket. I greeted her and her team at the dock after they clinched the gold. I cried when she stood on the podium and received her medals. Her victory was symbolic for me. Symbolic of her triumph over breast cancer, and that moment was a celebration of living life fully.

I kept thinking about her and the impact she'd had on me for the rest of our trip. I was so amazed to see a survivor go on with their life, being active and fun and happy. I sent her a postcard to say how much our meeting meant to me. And she sent me an email saying the same thing.

By January, we had developed the most amazing friendship through email conversations. We shared the nitty gritty awful stuff about breast cancer. And we shared other aspects of our lives since all of those experiences are interwoven. By February, we decided that we'd like to write a book and share our experiences with others.

And here it is. A book that is bigger than either one of us. A project that seemed destined to be way before we met, and maybe even before either of us was diagnosed with breast cancer.

How the Book Came to be

From: Megan
Sent: February 5, 2003

I do have to share this idea. I've been wanting to write some kind of breast cancer book that would be of value. I haven't figured out exactly what the content would look like. I'm thinking that we are compiling a lot of great material with our emails. Maybe 10 years out, when it's not quite so painful, we could write a book together. We could do Oprah together. Of course, we change names to protect everyone (mostly us) and cut anything we feel like cutting. In flipping through my journal, I found the name I came up with months ago that seems to support the email compilation, "So, you think you are done? A guide to surviving breast cancer when treatment ends." Could be a way to create our own life insurance.

From: Meredith
Sent: February 5, 2003

Love the idea of the book - I was going to suggest much the same thing myself. I got sick of people giving me naff books while I was sick about how to cure yourself of cancer by following the perfect diet and giving up sailing and anything else that was fun. I resolved that I was going to write a book titled, "How I Cured my Cancer by Drinking Champagne, Eating Fattening Food and Traveling to Italy".

I never really made any progress with it - probably because the topic was all still too raw, but also I think through our joint email exchanges we are finding a really unique perspective on things that would be a stronger book anyway.

Honestly I think there are probably a lot of other women out there who feel the same way about all of this as we do, but don't have anyone with the same viewpoint to talk about it with - I mean, we didn't until we met. I can see us now on Oprah's Book of the Month!

Our Point...and we do have one!

Usually when people are sad, they don't do anything.
They just cry over their condition.
But when they get angry,
they bring about a change.

MALCOLM X

Cancer is so overwhelming and so out of the range of any individual's experience, that when we were diagnosed we both looked actively for role models and resources to help us make sense of what we were experiencing and how to cope.

And although we did come across some extraordinary individuals and useful books, none really matched what we were feeling in the moment and our attitude towards life. At the time in the back of both of our minds was the thought that one day we should each write our own book on how to cope with breast cancer.

Despite that thought, we never got started. It wasn't until we met and started working through the impact of this illness on our lives with the support of each other that we began to clarify the key learnings from our experience and what would be most important to share.

The many email conversations we had shared about the hard stuff became our starting point. When we actually had the opportunity to spend time together again and discuss issues in more detail, the book you are holding began to take shape.

This book is based on a collection of email exchanges, transcripts of live conversations and separate essays we wrote at different stages of our journey. It is episodic in nature, because we focused on key points in our experience that we wanted to explore.

It isn't chronological, because one of the most important things we learned is that this journey is not linear. During diagnosis, treatment and, most importantly, when learning to go on with life afterwards, there are moments of great clarity and insight and moving forward, and those days when things just all fall apart. The key is to keep putting one foot in front of the other.

In writing the book, we discovered some major themes that we wanted to share, and which wind through the conversations on every topic:

How the Heck Do I Cope with This?

Without consciously thinking about and choosing coping strategies, there are things we did during our journey that helped us to make it through the day and keep our momentum, even when things got really hard.

Setting short and long term goals, keeping good things in life, giving ourselves rewards to look forward to, creating reasons to get up out of bed and keep moving - whether it was going to the gym or visiting family - all helped to keep us on track.

Living Life Fully

One of our greatest frustrations after diagnosis was the feeling that someone or something had put restrictions on our life for the first time. We focused on continuing to do the things that were important to us in our lives, and then looked at those things we hadn't done that were important to us, and found a way to make them happen.

Whatever You Choose is OK

Going through the experience of cancer, we found that there is a lot of pressure around choosing your treatment options and in deciding what lifestyle changes should be made, if any.

At a time when you are most vulnerable and scared, you have to make decisions about your health that are far reaching in terms of surgery and further treatment regimes and it is a struggle to maintain your power and be your best advocate.

And there is all the pressure from outside to adopt radical lifestyle changes in the hope it may impact your future prognosis.

We learned how important it is to be a strong advocate, or to find a strong advocate for your health and treatment. And, at the end of the day there is no right or wrong way to cope with a diagnosis of cancer.

Everyone needs to find their own best way forward, learning from other people's experiences, and making your own choices.

Technology and Community

We were fortunate to be diagnosed in an age not only of incredible medical technology, but also communications technology.

Dealing with cancer by yourself can be an overwhelming and daunting exercise, and everyone's experience is different. Finding someone with whom you can connect and feel supported by can be difficult.

Also, dealing with the needs of those around you at a time that your mental and spiritual resources are stretched can be incredibly challenging.

Email played a huge role for us in providing a safe medium for us to get to know each other and eventually discuss the really hard stuff, but also as a key communication tool for our friends and family in updating them on where we were, without a drain on our energy.

The ability of email and the web to build community across great distances is enormous. One of our future goals is developing a web site for breast cancer survivors to help them find the same support. No one should go through this journey alone.

Medical Professionals

When we were diagnosed we found ourselves immersed in a medical world outside our experience. We were very fortunate to have some great doctors, nurses and other health professionals to guide and support us at various stages of our treatment.

Unfortunately, we also had some really negative experiences when the system in which we were caught did not seem equipped to handle our emotional needs.

We hope this book provides some insights to the medical profession about the emotional roller coaster their patients are riding, and how little things that are done through treatment can make a huge difference in their experiences.

Our Journeys

*I think that wherever your journey takes you,
there are new gods waiting there,
with divine patience - and laughter.*

SUSAN M. WATKINS

Australia's Breast Cancer Day Speech October 2002
by Meredith Campbell

This story is about journeys - physical journeys, emotional journeys, and spiritual journeys.

September 2000 was a pretty heady month. The Olympics were on in Sydney, Australians were winning just about everything in sight. Some of my friends were competing as members of the Australian Team in Sailing.

I was 33 years old, had a 6 year old son, and was at the peak of my profession. The following month I was due to travel to India to visit programs I had helped fund working with disadvantaged rural women and children. In November, I was due to go to London to speak at an International Conference.

Life was pretty damned good. And then on the day that Australia won its first ever gold medals in women's sailing, I was diagnosed with breast cancer. Twenty-four hours later I was recovering from surgery and spent my weekend watching the closing ceremony of the Games from my hospital bed.

My plans for traveling were pretty well shot - I was told that within a couple of weeks I would start three months of chemotherapy, followed by three months of radiation treatment, and then another three months of chemo.

Of all of the emotions that I went through at that time, the strongest were of anger and grief. For the first time in my life someone or something had tried to put limitations on me.

I was young and fit and I thought I was going to live forever. And even having made it through treatment and still being well, I can never look at my life going forward in the same way again.

Straight after surgery I sat down to read all the literature, including that on lymphedema, of which I was at risk in my left arm. There was a whole list of things one should avoid doing in order to reduce your risk.

Top of the list was vacuuming. I can happily report - two years, no vacuuming, no lymphedema!!! That's what I call a clinical trial.

Unfortunately the list also had things on it like not carrying heavy weights, not having strain on that arm for a significant period of time, not getting sun burnt...all the things you generally do when you go sailing.

I spoke with the staff at the hospital and their physio and was told, "Oh no, you won't be able to sail again." Once again people trying to put limitations on me.

After a week of ringing around we finally found a physio who was prepared to work with me. After getting my shoulder moving again, she stuck with me developing a gym program so I could keep working out through chemo, and fixing the myriad of things that kept going bung as my treatment progressed.

Just as I was ready to start my second round of chemo, I was offered the opportunity to travel to San Francisco for a conference. My oncologist didn't need too much persuading to let me go, and I boarded the plane two weeks to the day after my first shot of Taxol.

The only problem was I knew from experience that would be the day my hair (having grown back reasonably during radiation) would be due to fall out. My boss who was traveling with me and who was follically challenged himself had happy fantasies of falling asleep over Hawaii and waking up with my hair!

I packed it full of product, and made it to the hotel with it reasonably intact, before losing it all down the drain in the shower. I have to complement San Francisco as a town because the concierge didn't bat an eyelid at having someone book in at 3 p.m. with hair and appear an hour later bald.

Not to mention that if you are going to be a bald woman anywhere in the world, San Francisco is guaranteed not to be surprised and in the right quarters you will be downright popular!

Five weeks after finishing my second round of chemo I boarded a plane to India to visit the programs I had helped fund working with poor children and women in the south - the same trip I had postponed a year earlier when I was diagnosed.

At that stage I had about two mm of hair grown back - devastatingly all grey! I have no idea if it's still grey and have no intention, thanks to Clairol, of finding out!

Most of the kids I was visiting had the same hairstyle and I had great fun pantomiming to them how cool it was we had the same cut. Until one of the staff explained to me that the kids couldn't work out if I was a Buddhist nun or just had head lice like them!

That trip was amazing to me, because whatever difficulties I had faced over the past year, it was nothing compared to the hardships these women and children faced with dignity and hope on a daily basis.

When I got home I followed through on another long held ambition - to get my motorcycle license and buy a bike! This kept me on the road and busy while preparing for my next challenge - traveling to Florida in April 2003 for the Avon 3-Day Walk for Breast Cancer.

As a professional fundraiser, I'd always been impressed by this fabulous event and had wanted to visit it to learn more. Now I had a personal reason to attend as well.

On 19th April 2002, I lined up with 3,000 other women to begin a marathon 60 mile/100 km walk over three days to raise funds for breast cancer. The weather was gorgeous for the beach but not for walking!

The temperatures were so high that by the time I arrived at the lunch stop on the first day I was greeted by the sight of a line of ambulances. The triage tent had 8 IVs hooked up to people who had become dehydrated. We found out at camp that night 6 people had been taken to hospital on the walk that day alone. Another two collapsed in the showers that night. This was a seriously tough physical event.

The walk was incredibly hard physically and an emotional rollercoaster - around 200 survivors walked in the group, and everyone else had a deep personal connection to the cause. When we finally reached Miami on the last day we were told the walk had netted an incredible $1.8 million dollars.

At the same time, we were told that on the three days we had walked, 245 women had died in the United States from the disease.

This week I am starting on a new journey with new challenges. I've just left the charity I have worked with for the last 8 years to establish my own consultancy business. I have a brand new motorbike due for delivery next week, and next month I will travel to London to give the presentation I was due to give two years ago.

I don't believe that there is a right way, or a wrong way to deal with a diagnosis of breast cancer and its impact on your life. I did what worked for me - and anyone in this situation has to find their own way to move forward.

If there is a moral or wisdom that I would share from my experiences, it would be to not accept the limitations that others or the disease may try to impose on you.

As I move forward on the next stage of my journey, I live by the words of the American poet, Walt Whitman.

Henceforth
I whimper no more
Postpone no more
Need nothing...
Strong and content
I travel the open road.

"Why I do Triathlons", Newsletter Article June 2003
by Megan Dwyer

I always wanted to be an athlete, and yet never did much about it. I was in the marching band in high school rather than sports. I did play water polo in college and loved it. After graduating, the challenges of becoming an "athlete" seemed even greater if not down right impossible. After all, there are not a lot of adult water polo recreational leagues.

While vacationing in Kona a couple of weeks before the Ironman Triathlon in 1991, I found myself fascinated by people training for what sounded like an insane event. Completing that event would definitely qualify you as an athlete. I bought a T-shirt and started dreaming.

I completed my first triathlon in June 1992 - the Danskin in San Jose. It was a sprint distance (short) triathlon for women only that raised funds and awareness for breast cancer. I completed it with a tequila hang over and can't say I was completely serious about it. I remember being inspired by all the survivors who were doing the Triathlon to challenge themselves and to somehow celebrate being alive.

I spent the next 10 years doing one or two tris a year. Never getting very serious. Never making it past an Olympic Distance. Never feeling like a real athlete. I'd avoided joining the Silicon Valley Triathlon Club since its inception, although I kept close tabs on the progress of the club. I kept thinking I'd join when I was a real athlete. I finally joined last year and made it to my very first track workout in June, 2002. I was training for the San Jose International Triathlon, and decided it was time to get a little more serious about my workouts.

Two days after the track workout, I was diagnosed with breast cancer. I was 35. I finally knew I was an athlete when 1) my first thought was that I never wanted to compete in the Danskin Triathlon as a survivor, 2) I tried to schedule my surgery around the San Jose International Triathlon and 3) I was more concerned about my presurgery resting heart rate than the procedure itself.

Once I started treatment, I soon learned where the "survivor" term comes from. It's a struggle. A struggle to keep going emotionally and physically. A struggle to remain positive. A struggle to not give up. A struggle to not long for the things you can no longer do. And there really is no choice but to go on...and to survive.

I had started a new career in real estate two months before I was diagnosed. I got my first listing two weeks before my diagnosis. I managed to put together the contract for that sale the weekend before my surgery. I cannot claim that I worked full time during my 5 months of recovery and treatment, but I took care of my clients and took baby steps toward building a successful business.

I faced one of my biggest challenges when I lost my hair to chemo. In sales, appearance can seem like everything. How could I possibly meet with clients? I did what most women do, I purchased a wig. And I hated it. It did not look like me. And it was hot. Really hot since it was July in Northern California. I couldn't stand it, and I eventually decided to just be myself. At this point of my life, that meant being bald, no matter how difficult that was for me.

I found my clients to be very supportive, and I think it may have even worked to my advantage in negotiations with other real estate agents! It also turned out to be effective in the world of triathlon as my competition thought I had merely shaved my head as a form of intimidation.

I missed the San Jose International Triathlon due to surgery. I refused to think in terms of limitation or slowing down, and I focused instead on my next two goals for the year. Getting through 3 months of chemo and competing in a sprint triathlon in Sydney, Australia in November as part of the Gay Games celebration. I managed both.

It was 110 degrees (42C) for the tri, which was held at the rowing venue for the 2000 Olympics. I had finished chemo 5 weeks before, was on a rented hybrid bike that took more effort to get my hands on than completing the race, and I had trained only as a serious couch potato for 6 months. I finished the tri in 1 hour and 58 minutes, just under my personal goal of 2 hours. And, I did not finish last, which I considered to be a major accomplishment.

I learned that day what makes me tri...I do it for the personal challenge. To push myself and find out what I am really capable of. To feel strong and powerful and unstoppable. To have the opportunity to hang out with some of the most fit athletes in the world. To know that I am fully alive and participating in the best life has to offer.

Because I am an athlete and a survivor.

Part II:

Diagnosis and Treatment

Diagnosis

Nothing travels faster than the speed of light
with the possible exception of bad news,
which obeys its own special laws.

DOUGLAS ADAMS

In this world of instant communication, it seems the fastest (and safest) way of communicating the news of diagnosis to friends and family is through email.

Meredith's Diagnosis Email

From: Meredith
Sent: Tuesday October 3, 2000

Hi All!

Rumors of my death have been greatly exaggerated. (I always wanted to use that line!).

By now some of you may have noticed I haven't been around for a few days (at least I hope you noticed!). Contrary to popular opinion I have not skipped the country or run off with the gypsies.

On Thursday last week I was diagnosed with breast cancer and on Friday night I was in surgery.

The operation went well and in a couple of weeks I will be starting a fairly long period of treatment -

three months of chemotherapy, followed by three months of radiation treatment, and then another three months of chemo.

I will be working through my treatment and expect to be in the office as often as possible, and working from home in between.

While obviously the whole cancer thing is a bit of a bummer, there are some positive aspects:

1. I finally get to have the Annie Lennox hair cut I wanted when I was 18!
2. I get tattooed! (Just little ones for when I have radiation treatment, but tattoos none the less!)
3. I can get new Lara Croft sized breasts on my health insurance.
4. Saving a fortune in hair product for the next 10 months.
5. My hair should grow back darker and curly which after several years of slowly emerging grey, will also save a fortune on hair colour and product.
6. No waxing for 10 months!
7. Losing weight from the nausea during chemo!
8. Getting to ditch the suits and work at home in my tracky daks and boardies.
9. Never having to vacuum again - its true! The doctor said so!
10. The perfect excuse to miss work and lie around and watch the last few days of the Olympics!

I know that many of you would like to call and offer your support - we really appreciate your good thoughts and wishes but at the moment John and I are focusing on family and organising my treatment. I will be in the office to see you all and catch up as soon as I am able.

Cheers
Meredith

Megan's Diagnosis Email

From: Sharon
Sent: Thursday, June 06, 2002

Dear Friends,

Yes, that means you. I am writing with some challenging and unexpected news. Megan has been diagnosed with breast cancer and will soon be starting treatment. We don't have many details and will not have additional information until they perform surgery and can "see" what's happening inside.

I am writing to ask for your prayers and well wishes and thoughts and words of support. As you can imagine, this news has come as a bit of a surprise. is NOT welcome news and is rather ch⁻''
handle. We both believe in the amaz'
of thoughts and prayers and wish
positive thoughts and prayers fo'
recovery.

All of you know me, so you w⸍
suggest an organized approa
humbly ask that we all sen⸍
gratitude and of hope to th
god/goddess before/as yo
that if we all did this aro⸍
have an abundant "store

through the night as her body rests and heals. So, if you're game, I thank you in advance for your participation.

I know that Megan would love to hear from you and hear your positive thoughts and hear any inspirational stories/experiences that you would be willing to share. So, please feel free to pick up the phone and let her know that you're thinking of her and wishing her outstanding health and energy. Thank you!

-Sharon and Elliott

Meredith's Diagnosis:
Live Conversation - California, June 2003

Megan: How did you initially find it?

Meredith: Ah! It was weird because there was probably stuff going on...well, there is a tendency to sort of look back and think, "Well, you obviously weren't well then and something was going on with your system." I worked way too hard. I worked really long hours. I worked weekends. I was working all the time. It's just the way I go about things, which will be no surprise to you. I'm much better now. I'm a recovering workaholic.

I was just really tired, and John and I went to Italy in May of that year and we had a fabulous time four weeks there. But as just tired all the time. I thought I ust overworked. So, I had to have an a couple of hours every afternoon. aving a pretty good time over retrospect the tiredness was unusual. Then I had weird stuff going on. I went down to Canberra for this big function with the Prime Minister and I had a dizzy spell and nearly fainted. I'd never had that in my life. Nose bleeds. I'd never had them before. So something odd was going on. I went to see my doctor. He checked my blood pressure and it was really low. Why that would cause me to have nose bleeds I don't know. He just thought it was overwork.

So, September was the middle of the Olympics. It's so hot in Queensland at that time of year and I just woke up in the middle of the night itching with an itch and scratched and thought, "Oh. What's that? That shouldn't be there." This big hard lump. And knew that it wasn't right. That it shouldn't be there. And I couldn't get back to sleep. I ended up getting up out of bed and surfing the internet for a few hours from about 3:00 in the morning. John finally wandered out a couple of hours later and I said, "I've found this lump and it doesn't seem right." And I said, "Have you noticed this?" He said, "Yea, well...I did." But h
So, he hadn't thought a

And things always se
the morning, especia
obsessive-compulsi
organized to see m
left work to see hi
straight off for a
sound. And I ha
there's lots of "

on. And I go for the ultrasound and there's lots of "umming and ahhing" going on. And then they stuck a needle in the thing. They did a fine needle biopsy.

Megan: All in the same day?

Meredith: All at the same time.

Megan: Oh my God!

Meredith: At which time I am thinking, "This is unusual."

Even though I'd had something benign taken out of my other breast when I was 16. I thought, "This isn't how it happened last time." They had a lot of trouble getting anything out of it with the needle. So the guy with the needle said, "Well, maybe it's fibrous or something since it's so hard to get something out of it. Whatever it is, it's going to have to come out." I thought well, fair enough. Been there, done that. It's just a scar.

He gave me the mammogram results or whatever to take back to my doctor who wanted to see me straight afterwards. He's really good. So I went back and I'm sitting there thinking, "What's the next question they usually ask you in this situation? Medical history." I knew one of my grandmothers, my paternal grandmother had breast cancer, really, really late - like in er eighties when you are going to get thing that's going anyway. Also my n that side had had breast cancer ian cancer.

So I rang my sister Suzanne who works in the breast cancer area to find out because I wasn't sure exactly what the history was and exactly what they had. I told her what the deal was and she said, "I'll be straight there." She was there in 10 minutes flat, before I even went in to see the doctor.

And of course she had a look at the x-ray while she was sitting there! She can't help herself. And he said we wouldn't know until we got the results from the fine needle biopsy, and that will probably be tomorrow. Suzanne had a look at it and she...she didn't think it looked that bad. She said normally with breast cancer it's usually pretty nasty, star shaped spread ing odd things, and this was very self-contained.

I was still reasonably uptight so obviously I didn't go back to work that day and just blew work off. The next day John went to work and Suzanne said she'd come over since we were expecting the call from the doctor at about 10:00 a.m. or so. And the doctor called about 10 minutes before she got there. It was my local doctor to say that he'd got the results and he was sorry, it was breast cancer. And I would need to speak with a surgeon. Suzanne and I had discussed it the night before and she knew a really good breast cancer surgeon. I mean regardless of what it was, it would have to come out.

She said you need to go and see this guy...he'd be really good. We had already discussed that and so I told him that my sister had referred me on to a surgeon and that I had that under control. I think I managed to handle the call reasonably well. I was as close as you can get to a panic attack when I hung up.

Megan: So you actually took the call from your doctor, and you were home alone at that point?

Meredith: Yeah.

So I just paced up and down the house and I was concentrating on just breathing calmly and not hyperventilating at the time. And thinking, "Oh F***. Oh F***. Oh F***." Then Suzanne was coming up the back stairs - the way our house is laid out that's where you normally come in - there's windows above them so you can see people coming to that door. She looked through the window and said, "Hello.", and she saw the look on my face and said, "What happened?" I said, "He just called and it's cancer." I just completely lost it...and broke down then. In as much as an analytical, introvert can I think. Or as much as I ever have. For about a minute.

And...got it under control enough to ring John and tell him, "You need to come home. The doctor has called and it's not good." So John came home. I think I was just completely off the planet. I was under reasonable control until John came home then I just lost it again. All I could say was, "I'm so sorry."

So Suzanne did what anyone would do in our family and went to the Italian deli to get champagne. More wine, good food...

Megan: What were you sorry about? Why were you saying, "I'm sorry."?

Meredith: I don't know. I think for me it has always been more about John than it has been about me. Really. In about being sorry about what the impact would be on him and our son Dexter. I've really not got such an issue about my own mortality which also is where I'm tied into... spirituality...there's either a place you go when you die or not and either way it's not an issue for you. You're dead, you're dead.

But the hardest thing for me has always been about how John and Dexter would cope afterwards. And that was something I couldn't get to. I ended up having to go and talk to a psychologist about it.

Dexter was over at...well it was school holidays and I was working so Dexter was at Mum and Dad's and what we worked out, cause I needed to...I just wanted it out...I wanted it gone Now. So that was Thursday and Suzanne rang the surgeon she'd recommended and he organized his schedule so that he could do it that Friday night. So I'd be straight in. And I didn't want to talk to my mother...and have to deal with it all. So Suzanne left John and me to sort of deal with it and went off to tell Mum and to organize for Dexter to sleep over while I was in hospital and all.

After I got over the initial overwhelming emotion of it, I was quite out of it. The Olympics were on and it was the day that Australia won two gold medals in sailing, including the two girls in the 470 winning the first ever women's medal. So we just put the sailing on and we drank beer. Suzanne was really good. She rang her husband Bert and then Bert rang my sister Julie and her partner Jules. And it was a while before they could call. Well, Julie rang and said Jules couldn't ring because she was crying. She was really upset about it. It took her a while.

But I think I was into the overcompensating stage by then because I had already had my pitch about how cool it would be. I had always wanted to do the Annie Lennox hair thing and you know my great chance to get Lara Croft boobs on my health insurance. I'd had a few beers by that stage.

I rang my boss and told him what was going on and said, "I'm not going to be back at work and I don't want to talk to anyone. Just fend them all off and when I am ready, I'll let them know something."

Yeah…so that was it. I really just think that I was not rational. I was just in shock and coping. I read an article about Breast Cancer Day back home where they talked to women about their reactions at the same time. One woman was a teacher and was actually at work when she got the call from her doctor. And she picked up and went golfing for the rest of the afternoon. Whatever you can do to distract yourself that has some semblance of normalcy, or anything other than dealing with the situation.

So, Dexter slept over at Mum's, and the next morning John went to work in the morning and Suzanne came over and took me shopping to get pajamas for hospital. We live in a tropical climate so I don't do pajamas. I know, too much information - I'll stop there! We went to Kmart and bought Dexter some really cool new toys and went over to see him. That took a while to get to the point where I could do that and deal with my Mum. And Dexter was just his usual self. "Let's watch television." So I sort of got through that and checked into hospital that night.

Then into hospital on the Friday night and checked in for the surgery and Suzanne came in and took John down to the pub downstairs. By the time I came out of recovery, they were still there. I got back to the room and they weren't there but I was too drugged to care. Then, 20 minutes later they went to recovery and found out I was already back in my room and go running up there and I was like, "Oh, OK you're here now..." And I spent another two days in the hospital watching the Olympics on television until I got to go home. And Dexter got to come and visit and that was kind of cool.

So...yeah....your turn!!

Megan's Diagnosis:
Live Conversation - California, June 2003

Meredith: It's like that seminar you went to where you had to come up with something you found really upsetting and you tell the story over and over until it doesn't hurt anymore. See, that's where I've gotten to now. After 2 1/2 years, the more you go through it, the easier it is to do without getting so emotional. That doesn't mean you have to do it now...

Megan: If I had that story here, I would just read it because that one is safe. It was Memorial Day, which is one of our very few holidays you know. Unlike the Australians who have a holiday every week.

Meredith: Ah, it's tough being an Australian.

Megan: And...Sharon noticed it. She said, "I don't want to scare you, but there is this lump and it just doesn't feel right." I had to agree. It didn't feel right. I think I slept that night, although I don't really remember. It was a Saturday night of a holiday weekend, so we couldn't really do anything until Tuesday. We had to wait a couple of days. And on Tuesday, Sharon got me an appointment with somebody. It didn't really matter who, but I had to get in to see somebody. Whoever this doctor was, she ordered a mammogram and ultrasound right away. It wasn't that day, but it was within a day or two.

I went in for the mammogram and then they had me wait and they went to see...if it turned out. And they said, "OK we are going to take you in for the ultrasound." Just the way they said it, you know, it didn't seem quite right. So, I went in for the ultrasound and...you can't tell anything. They won't tell you anything. I just wasn't getting a good vibe out of anybody.

After that was done, I was pretty shaken, but we still didn't know anything. Then they decided that I needed to do the needle biopsy. It was the big one, not the little one. The small needle biopsy sounded better! And that was another couple of days away. I think it was the following Tuesday. I think it had been a full week.

I got Dr. Susan Love's Breast Health book, which was helpful. I had to be careful not to read too far ahead because I didn't want to know too much, but I was glad it talked about the large needle biopsy because it was terrifying. You go in and there is a hole in the table and you lay face down, and your breast goes through the hole, and they mammogram it. They flatten it, they yank it through the table and they squish it.

It was the most miserable, uncomfortable thing you can imagine. The x-ray was instantly visible on the computer screen so they can locate the lump exactly. Then the doctor came in and shot this large needle in, which took out a pretty good core - maybe 1/16th inch cores. They took like, 10 of them.

They numbed my breast and then "blip, blip, blip" all the way around the whole thing. And then they showed me after-wards. It was like this little tray of what looked like little worms.

Meredith: Oh, like you really needed to see that!

Megan: It was awful. "Thanks so much." And when he left he said, "Good luck." I didn't feel real good about that.

When I came out of that appointment, Sharon had...I don't know what they said in terms of timing, but they did it in half the time they were supposed to. So Sharon had gone to get something. When I came out, I was pretty shaken, and she wasn't there. I had this stupid ice pack in my bra and it hurt like hell, and I was really upset and was kind of wandering around the hospital looking for her. I think I probably gave her a little lecture on never leaving me because...when I had foot surgery when I was 19, my parents had disappeared. They swear to this day that they went to get flowers for me. So I kind of had some issues about being abandoned while being cut in the hospital.

Then we had to wait a couple of days. It was Thursday. The biopsy was Tuesday and Thursday we actually got a call. We were sitting at home with a loan officer because we were looking at refinancing our house. So the call came and Sharon went outside and took the call, and we just kept talking to this guy. Although I was definitely distracted. As soon as he left, she said, "It's not good. It's breast cancer."

Meredith: That must have been hard to continue that conversation after that call.

Megan: Well, what could we do? We had this guy in our home, talking about loans and loan rates and such, and we just got this awful news.

Let this guy go away, get out of here. And then we can fall apart.

And that's what happened. When he left, it was noon. I remember because it was just in time to have a drink! I was shaken. I had a friend in college who when anything would happen she would talk about trembling. I always thought, "What the hell makes you tremble in life?" That's what came to mind first, was wow, I'm trembling. That was the first out of control sign. And I was totally pacing because I had all this energy. Like, "What the F***!"

Meredith: Like coping with an adrenaline reaction. And you're pacing...

Megan: I was thinking about that pacing. I've got...the same energy is coming out now. It's like I have to do something, but what do I do? There is nothing to do. There is nothing you can do in that instance, and it is the most helpless, frustrating, overwhelming feeling. Really, I couldn't think. All I said was, "You'd better get me a drink." So we opened a bottle of wine. Then I thought, "Gee, I never wanted to be a survivor at those stupid triathlons." Literally that thought was within the first 10 minutes.

Then we called my Mom and my sister Shannon, and they came over.

Mom was at work. Sharon spoke with her and said, "Can you come over? We just got the test results back and its breast cancer." And she started crying on the phone. And she said, "I'll be right there." We found out later that apparently she was just so upset that her coworkers were worried about her, so one of them got in a car and followed her to our house to make sure she got there safely.

My sister Shannon left work too. And then they called a family friend, whose daughter is our goddaughter. They drove over and brought bags of chocolate and chips and all kinds of wonderfully distracting junk food.

I started crying and saying, "I'm sorry." The same thing as you.

Afterwards I thought I had just gone through all the emotions you possibly could in that one day, while being drunk. Which would be the way the safest way to do it. Little did I know that I would actually have to go through them again in real time.

I just went out on the balcony and went through some of the stuff you talked about. That basically I had had an amazing life, and I had no regrets at all about how I'd lived my life. If that was the end then I really couldn't complain. But I felt really sad and scared about leaving Sharon, and my nieces came to mind. They were both under the age of two. For me to not be around for them growing up...that was the hardest thought. I figured everyone else could figure out how to cope. And even they have parents and would be all right.

So, I kind of went through all of that, and the denial and the pissed off. I just did my own little microcosm of emotions. And people were really good and left me alone and did their own coping in the house, and just let me be insane, basically. Then I puked my guts out on the balcony and we hosed it all off later. And by 10:00 p.m. I was sober again. Then I was like, "Now what?"

That was a long day.

Sharon wrote an email to just let people know and to just ask for good wishes and the belief that all good energy helps, so send it our way.

I think Sharon started making calls to doctors that day. I don't remember. I couldn't tell you. I was not really available for that. If not that day, then the next. We had a few options in terms of surgeons.

At first they wanted to have me see this doctor three weeks out.

Meredith: Oh, no! I don't think so.

Megan:	No. So we called until we found a doctor who was willing to do everything in her power to expedite. She just kept calling around and pushing on our behalf and getting back to us. She was very helpful in that way. She was very helpful in getting us talking with the right people and explaining the two options we had at that hospital. Both great doctors. The thing that turned it for us is I talked with the nurses of both surgeons and one of them just seemed like she was willing to work with me, and tried to calm me down a little bit and to explain.
	And, as we found out more about this doctor whose nurse I liked, it turned out that this doctor insisted on her patients staying overnight, which apparently is not typical.
Meredith:	I can't believe that.
Megan:	The other surgeon just sends them home the same day. So when we heard this part we said, "Yes. This is definitely the right surgeon."
	Before we met with the surgeon, the clinic that I went to has a breast cancer nurse who will meet with you. She does breast cancer counseling for women who have just been diagnosed.
	So Shannon and Sharon and Mom and I went in and we spent two hours with her and you could ask anything and she had her little charts and the various treatments,

and she was just one of those really incredible people. Just a real sweetheart. And it really helped to talk. We threw questions at her left and right.

I came out of there knowing what was going on. I knew what the options were and what the odds were and I just felt really comfortable. Plus, she gave us the inside scoop. This doctor is like this and this doctor is like this, and who might be the best fit for you...I knew I had options, and that was pretty cool.

So, we met with the surgeon, and she was great. The biggest conversation was around what kind of treatment did I want. I had the option of lumpectomy or mastectomy. And I was a borderline case. It was definitely up to me.

But if I had the lumpectomy, I had to have radiation, and that just wasn't going to work with my schedule. I had the Gay Games coming up in Sydney, and I couldn't have gone if I'd done that. Also I had a triathlon I was trying to work around that was in June. Sharon was really pushing for an early surgery. She did a lot of negotiating to get it moved up.

I got in not in the three week timeframe they originally tried to stick us with, but much, much earlier. I took the first appointment they would give me for surgery. So I missed the triathlon, but it made Sydney more likely, which was a big consideration. We'd been planning for the thing for two years. So if there was any way around that.

I ended up having my surgery within three weeks of finding the lump.

The nurse was fantastic, and helped us all the way through. She recommended this surgicenter. It was awesome. I had a choice between Stanford and the surgicenter, and the surgicenter just sounded pretty cool, so that's where we ended up.

We suspect that's where all the rich women go for plastic surgery.

And so I showed up, and they checked me in, and it was really nice and really comfortable. They took me back to my room, which looked like a hotel room. It had a double bed, carpet. It had a pull out sofa for your overnight guest. Fridge, armoire, TV, VCR... And we had people coming through. My surgery was in the morning and the room across the hall had donuts and coffee for my visitors.

It was amazing. And I was wired and ready to go. And I was totally excited because my heart rate was something like 49, and I thought, "Cool! I'm finally in shape." Not that it lasted. One odd thing was that they made me put a band-aid on the breast to be removed - just to be sure they get the right one and if they screwed up, it would be my fault.

The surgicenter was really, really comfortable and everybody came, and I got to walk down the hall to the operating room. And they had this heated operating table. It was all warmed up, and I got on and it was really comfortable. They did every thing so incredibly well. It felt like I was in for a massage.

I woke up and Sharon and my niece Iman were outside the door. I was still in the recovery room, looking out, and they were out there waving and talking. It was so funny. The surgery was only an hour and a half or so. Something really short. They wheeled me back to my room and there were all these people and Sharon and Mom.

Then they all went shopping at some point, and Sharon crawled in bed with me and we watched World Cup soccer. Then everyone came back, and you know you are kind of in and out of it. I was in pretty good shape, but taking naps and visiting and taking a nap and a little shot of morphine.

Iman was…there is something about having a little baby there where it is like nothing is wrong. They want you to get up and walk around, and she was the one pushing my IV tree.

Everybody stayed. I think it was 10:00 or 11:00 p.m. when they finally left. Sharon spent the night on the sofa bed, and we went home in the morning. It was great.

Meredith: The fact that you went home the next day…I had my surgery and I was doing that in and out, in and out thing most of the rest of the day. They wouldn't let me leave until the drain was taken out. They wouldn't take it out until there was only a certain amount of fluid. So I was there for three nights. But I was just fading in and out for most of the rest of the day.

Megan: I remember…being an over achiever…I remember getting dressed…

Meredith: I didn't actually get out of bed for 24 hours, and you are up and going places with your IV tree.

Megan: I was up within two hours of surgery.

I remember the next day, getting up and getting dressed and being ready to go. Like an idiot. I was tired, but I thought I felt pretty darn good. I was really in over achiever mode. I was upset that I missed the triathlon. So this was like my version of the triathlon.

Meredith: Did you have to wear those awful surgery stockings?

Megan: They were awful. I was not even going to mention them.

Meredith: I haven't actually given a lot of thought to the whole thing. Is there no other indignity, I have to wear these revolting stocking things that are uncomfortable.

Megan: They were white and glow in the dark.

The worst part was waking up with the two tubes. They remove so much tissue that you get those stupid drainage tubes. I had my tubes for a week. And it was awful because we had to drain the darn things all week long.

We had to keep track of how much fluid was there to make sure it was decreasing as a sign my body was actually healing. I didn't want to do it. I made Sharon do it.

I just didn't want to deal with it. My surgery was Monday, and we went sailing on Saturday with those tubes hanging out of me. If we'd have had rough weather, I'd have been in big trouble. It was dead calm winds, and we motored the whole time. I had an open wound basically. My chest had been sliced open. The vibration from the motor was like biting nails or some thing. It was just awful.

Finally they took the tubes out. They were like two feet long.

Sharon watched them do it. It was the most disgusting thing. Here's the doctor, and she just starts pulling, and pulling, and pulling. Sharon said the worst part was when she looked at my chest and it was like one of those X Files things.

So she pulls out the first one and it just kept going and Sharon said, "Oh God!" And the doctor said, "OK. There's the short one." Sharon said, "Oh my God. The short one?" I wasn't looking, but I made some horrified noise or something and Sharon looked over at my face. I was looking really pale by then. It's such a bizarre feeling. Everything was so numb, it wasn't like anything hurt.

Meredith: But you know something is going on.

Megan: Yeah, it's creepy. I was just so glad they were out. A week of those things was gross.

Treatment:
Live Conversation - California, October 2003

Meredith: You've talked in the past about the conscious decisions you made about what kind of treatment you were going to have after surgery.

Megan: Yeah, for me it was like, maybe it's going to help, maybe it's not. I'm still struggling with that. I don't regret choosing that chemo, but theoretically they got it all with the surgery. The chemo was bonus treatment.

You don't know that going into the surgery, but after surgery that's how it turned out. It was self-contained in this little lump. That happened to be 3 mm from my chest. But, other than that.

Which is actually why I was glad I had the mastectomy, not the lumpectomy, because how do you know they got all of it when it is that close to the chest?

That was a hard decision for me because as a vegan I was in this world of, "If you eat the right way, you won't get it, and if you do get it you can do twenty other things. Eat this way and the cancer will go away."

I actually believed that could happen. And, it's not like I had no other options.

I had a pretty easily treatable, standard kind of a deal.

The doctors said that if I had chemo, I would have an 85% chance of being just like everybody else in terms of getting breast cancer again. It seemed stupid not to do it. But I had to talk to a lot of people to get to that point.

And especially with all the reasons why I'd been a vegan for so long. It was counter to all that. My thought was, "I'm going to intentionally put crap into my body that I know is going to do harm, and maybe there's a little, itty bitty chance it's going to add 5% to the chances that I'll live longer."

If I happen to be one of those people that this will make a difference for, then maybe it will make a difference but, if you go straight on statistics it didn't make sense to do it.

Meredith: The discussion I had with my surgeon beforehand was about likely scenarios. I definitely had to have chemo for some period of time, could be 3 months, 6 months, whatever.

And then I had the surgery and my lymph-nodes came back positive so I went off to see the medical oncologist and with my pathology results he said that the old chemo drugs wouldn't have worked for me anyway.

So, what they were recommending now was three months with a new drug, then

3 months of radiation and another three months of chemo with another drug.

I just said to him, "Go for it. Just nuke me. I want the strongest, the best drugs, whatever, I want as much as you can possibly give me to kill the damn thing."

He said to me, "Well, technically we don't refer to it as 'nuking'." I said, "I don't care, just go for it and do it." There was never any hesitation for me about I want the best possible drugs and as much of it as I can possibly have.

Reflecting back on the whole lumpectomy versus mastectomy decision, my surgeon said it wouldn't make that much difference. With the chemo, your chances would be much the same.

It wasn't really an issue for me - I just wanted the bloody thing out, now, and whatever he recommended - even mastectomy, would be fine with me.

Reconstruction at the time wasn't big on my agenda either - my surgeon said generally you wait a bit down the track to consider what can be done, and I wasn't particularly fussed about it at the time either.

I never saw it as a big choice, and I think I probably didn't really understand the ramifications of the choice between lumpectomy and mastectomy.

Megan: So how did you eventually make the decision?

Meredith: Well that was basically it - on the night, it was, "OK - that's what you recommend, let's do that." It was very quick - I was diagnosed that morning, in to the surgeon's office that night, made the decision and I was in surgery the following night.

Whatever he reckoned I was OK with. Suzanne was there and his recommendation fit with all her knowledge of the best possible options, so that's what we did.

I didn't see it as a big decision. If he'd said mastectomy was the way to go, that's what I would have done.

I've still had to deal with my issues about what I see as being lopsided, and awkward, and restricting what I can wear and me being more hyper-sensitive to that than other people who probably don't even notice.

However, going in for my check up this time around when they found more lumps and had to do biopsies I had to reconsider it all again.

This time there were lumps were on the side where I'd previously had surgery, whereas in my last check up scare they were on the right side.

So thinking about worst case scenarios, I had in my head that if it's back to the primary site they're hardly going to do lumpectomy again - if it's back there.

And thinking about the impact of having a mastectomy this time around was a much bigger prospect to deal with than I expected. It gave me more pause. More thinking about the impact of that decision than I had certainly done the first time around.

Now I may have more understanding of the impact of those choices, probably through my discussions with you, but it was definitely bigger this time around.

I don't know what choice I would make if I end up in that situation a second time around.

I've still got no intention of doing reconstruction because I'm not convinced I'm going to end up with a better outcome than I've currently got.

I certainly don't want any more surgery, and I'm not really keen on them moving bits of my anatomy from anywhere else and ending up with more side effects.

Megan: We had a bunch of discussions with the doctors about my specific case and they were pretty adamant that lumpectomy vs. mastectomy was equal for longevity. It didn't make a difference.

What tipped me over was that we knew it was near my chest. That kind of bothered me. We didn't know how close, but it was close enough to be a concern.

The other thing was in talking to my surgeon, was the question of, "How disfigured would you be with lumpectomy?" She figured it was going to be significant. Enough so that I said, "Well, what the heck is the difference? Just take the whole thing." It was a really easy decision for me.

With sports and athletics being such a priority it always seemed like it'd be easier without them anyway. I really didn't get the full impact of being lopsided at that time.

I have a really small chest and I just thought it would not be an issue at all. And it turned out to be a bigger issue than I imagined. I'm still really glad I made the decision I did, especially the way things worked out, but I do sometimes think I probably did have more choices than I thought at the time.

But the other piece that was really big for me was going to Australia, and radiation didn't fit in. The only way lumpectomy would have worked was if I had radiation and I didn't want to be bound for months having to go in every day.

That wouldn't fit in my schedule for 20 years! I didn't see how that was going to work at all. You can go have chemo and you can leave and do whatever you want, but having to be there every day for radiation wasn't working for me at all.

And I'd heard enough from people who'd had radiation and I really didn't want to feel fried and have the skin effects. Not that I thought it was going to leave any thing else but I just didn't want to have pieces that were more broken than they had to be.

I'm already doing surgery, and I'm already going to be cut up, so just take it all and then I don't have to do this extra piece.

I was still debating the whole chemo thing at that point.

I really wanted to do as little as possible to feel as safe as possible.

Meredith: Yeah, you know, I'm still a bit conflicted about it. I mean with my surgery I've still got some left, but it's still not the same and it's still always a reminder.

Megan: It's definitely not the same and it's definitely a reminder, and we have some pretty good jokes about it. I pretend I am all muscle on that side - like I've been working out.

There's something weird about having nothing there, you know, versus half of something. It's hard to describe the psychological impact.

Meredith: Either way, it's never the same. Even with reconstruction, it's not going to be the same.

Megan: In both cases, it's the same experience of loss, actually.

Prosthesis and Reconstruction

*As trapped, confused and afraid as you are,
it is important to remember that you do indeed
have choices.*

THOMAS MELOHN

From: Megan
Sent: Wednesday, February 05, 2003

Today's topic of discussion - my fake boob, affectionately known as "the prosthesis". I put off getting the thing as long as I could. I ran around Sydney asymmetrical for most of the trip. I especially loved it when they hosed me down after the triathlon - I was not prepared for the wet T-shirt look.

When I tried to be presentable, I had a bit of stuffing that Sharon made for me using cotton and bubble wrap (for a little stability).

The surgeon had given me some triple thick, heavy-duty camisole in July. Sharon and I completely fell apart laughing at the doctor's office when I tried it on - the "boob" it came with was huge. We removed stuffing and removed stuffing and laughed and laughed. I couldn't wear the stupid camisole in the middle of summer without suffering heat stroke. So I went around lopsided or stuck the bubble wrap version in my standard minimalist bra.

Only trouble with that was the off balanced weight and the tendency for the stuffing to slip around into very odd positions without me noticing. Plus, it was awfully hot to have bubble wrap plastered to your chest during the middle of summer.

When we got home, I broke down and went for the real thing. I think the Bay Area with its astronomical rates of breast cancer is one of the few places in the world with a shop that sells nothing but post-mastectomy bras. Thank goodness the woman who owned the shop was incredibly sweet and patient. She has people come in from all over the world with their makeshift boobs. She said she's seen rice and bird seed and who knows what else. I did not mention my bubble wrap.

Anyway, she tried various combinations of bras and boobs on me for an hour and a half. It was quite an ordeal. I don't think I've ever owned such a substantial bra in my entire life.

I have to be careful when I drink, because I have a strong desire to pull out my $350 boob and pass it around. It's pretty odd to have half your chest slide off each evening and spend the night in a drawer. It is pretty heavy and I often think it would be great for some sport.

When I am really ornery, I want desperately to chuck it against the wall hard enough for it to explode. Unfortunately, the insurance won't pay for another for two years.

I have no idea what the real number is, but it seems like most women who have mastectomies opt for reconstruction. It's almost assumed that you will. All of the support groups and informational things I went to soon after I was diagnosed had sessions on "Understanding Your Reconstruction Options".

I looked closely at the reconstruction options and thought they all sounded awful. One, they would take way too much time. They all involve more complex surgeries than the original mastectomy. And most involve multiple surgeries over several months. Two, I was really concerned about losing mobility or strength. I figured my chances of continuing with triathlons and other athletic activities was much higher if I kept the surgical procedures to a minimum. Honestly, some of the procedures horrified me. Really a huge trade off physically for a boob I thought.

So, the decision to skip reconstruction was pretty easy for me. And, the implications of that decision turned out to be bigger than I thought. I'm not sure what I thought. Just that it wouldn't be a big deal I guess. In the grand scheme of things, it isn't a big deal. But there are a whole lot of things that come up and bring it to my attention and fall into the quite annoying category. Like forgetting my special bra at the gym. Forgetting it is not so annoying as the fact that I have to have it.

Since I'm not that big, and I rarely wear anything that accents my chest, I figured I could get away without ever getting a prosthesis. I lasted about 6 months. I was pretty surprised to find how much the weight imbalance affected me. My posture, which was always pretty decent, went totally haywire. And my back was sore from trying to make up the difference. It also turned out that many of my clothes showed off more than I thought. Surprised the heck out of me that I actually cared if my chest looked at least roughly symmetrical.

So now I have my magical prosthesis. A pretty good compromise. It is incredibly comfortable. Puts me back to "normal" weight wise, which dramatically improves my posture and my back. But I really resent having to wear it. Especially now that it's summer. I always went without a bra all summer. Even in a baggy T-shirt, that doesn't really work anymore. I don't know what other people experience looking at me, but I am really self-conscious. Sometimes, when I am being particularly bold, I actually leave the house without a bra.

Other things seem to bug me too. Like showering at the gym. That was never my favorite activity before, but I did it. Now I have these panic attacks that some little kid is going to wander through and be traumatized for life. Although the thought of their parents having to explain it is pretty entertaining.

It also comes up for me at triathlons. I really don't want to mess with a prosthesis while racing. And my lack of symmetry is noticeable even in a wetsuit. Probably no one notices at all. And it is silly for me to be distracted at the start of a race by whether or not anyone has noticed. I wonder if there are any rules around a prosthesis as an illegal floatation device.

They have a prosthesis that attaches to your chest with velcro. I thought that would be pretty cool and very handy. Unfortunately, I am allergic to surgical tape (of all things) and so that model is not an option for me.

This part is kind of hard for me to share. Embarrassing for some reason. Every once in a while I'll have a sense of loss that is triggered by public toplessness. Like the Bay to Breakers run in San Francisco, or the Pride Parade. Not that I ever went topless at one of those, or had ever planned to. But, I always knew I could. I never thought I had the greatest breasts in the world, but they were perfect for me. A good size for being totally active. Never got in my way. Decent looking. Well balanced.

I suppose I could still do the topless thing if I was really inspired. Nothing to be ashamed of. But I'm not that well adjusted that I want to bare my chest to the world. I think it has to be uncomfortable for other people. Distracting at best.

Sometimes I think what a shame. What a waste. I didn't even know I was taking them for granted. I suppose a breast is one of the few body parts you can lose without having a huge functional impact. Still, it's sad. You go into surgery looking totally normal, feeling really excited to get the evil cancer removed. And you come out with such a huge piece of your body missing.

So, the prosthesis allows me to appear in the world as almost normal. Still kind of sucks, though.

From: Meredith
Sent: Monday, August 13, 2003

When I was diagnosed, like you, I really didn't have a big issue about whether it was going to be lumpectomy or mastectomy - I just wanted the damn thing out NOW!

In the end, my surgeon said the differences in survival rate with the triple whammy treatment regime I was in for were the same, so lumpectomy sounded fine - particularly as I was of the view the less surgery the better!

In terms of reconstruction then, the option was getting something done further down the line and I figured I'd see how I felt about it then.

Once I had the surgery in the first place, I had huge dramas with my shoulder locking up and a heap of physio to get things moving again. Hospital sucks, lets face it, and I wasn't really keen on the idea of having any more surgery at that point.

Then I got stuck with the great secondary of the belly button scare and had to go in and get that cut out. My surgeon does a great job with breasts, but I think even he wasn't overly impressed with the cosmetic results on my stomach - gone from a 6 pack to an asymmetrical two-pack!!!

That pretty much put the final nail in the coffin as far as reconstruction went for me.

Couldn't face the surgery, let alone the impact of that on other parts of my body, and I really am not convinced that they would have ended up with anything more symmetrical for me.

For a start, the radiation treatment I had changed the density of the breast tissue on that side - firmed it up nicely - almost like getting a breast lift. Maybe I should have gotten them to do both sides!

So what I'm left with now is a 3/4 pounder on one side that sits higher than the other one anyway because of the radiation and the surgery.
I also can't go without a bra in summer which is a major bummer because it gets so hot over here - having nipples that sit at completely different heights just doesn't work.

Although I can almost get away with it in a bra (at least as far as most people seem to tell me) I am totally conscious that in the tight T-shirts that are the mainstay of my wardrobe it is really noticeable to me. It's the first thing I saw in all the photos of us together in California.

I can totally relate to the shower thing at the gym! At the Avon Walk last year the shower trucks were smaller and there was a larger common area for changing. I thought that for once I'm not going to be the only lopsided one in here!

You know in some ways, with your prosthesis (especially the second one you got) you can get away with far more than me.

I'm stuck with bikinis because that's the only swimwear I can wear that hoiks them both up to approximately the same position. And I have to be careful what I do in it or things end up where they shouldn't!

With the exception of your acrobatics in the pool in Sonoma to find out just what it would take to get your prosthesis to pop out and float away, I think you have more options than me.

Plus that dress you got away with pinning your prosthesis into - the one with the spaghetti straps - I can't pull off anything like that at all!

So while I'm completely conscious of the fact that to me my lopsidedness is so noticeable, everyone who talks to me about it says they can't tell. And admittedly Sharon did end up asking which side I'd had the surgery on in Napa so maybe there is something to it!

I couldn't tell the heck whether you were wearing the prosthesis or not when you were wearing your baggy T-shirts in California, and I know for a fact you were not wearing it all the time because I distinctly remember learning to throw a football American style using your prosthesis in San Francisco!

And to be honest, you'd have to pay a lot of attention to notice when you were wearing your swimsuit without the prosthesis to notice. When you sent me the video of your triathlon at the Games I was wondering if you would have done it with a prosthesis - I know the video quality wasn't that great on my computer, but you really had to look hard to tell.

You know that every year over here (except this year because of funding problems) the Sydney Gay and Lesbian Mardi Gras parade is broadcast on national television.

I had exactly the same thought watching it the year after my surgery that you did when Dykes on Bikes came through. Now I would never have aspired to ride through the streets of Sydney topless on a bike, but my first thought was, "Well, that's something you'll never be able to get away with now."

I think it's one of those things we will always be more conscious of than everyone else, who really don't notice it. As you said, just one of those things we have to live with, but still a bit sucky though.

Chemo

Life shrinks or expands in proportion to one's courage.

ANAIS NIN.

Chemo:
Live Conversation - California, June 2003

Megan: OK, what are some of the worst things about chemo?

Meredith: Oh! Worst things about chemo....sitting for 2 1/2 hours to see your oncologist before you even got in for your chemo. Having nurses who couldn't do Veni puncture worth a damn.

Megan: Sitting there for hours while the nurses sorted out their medication. I don't know what they were doing. Getting called back because they gave you the wrong dosage. Back to back chemo sessions. That pretty much sucked.

Meredith: Having people take 4 or 5 goes at the veins in the back of your hand that don't hold up all that well anyway...

Megan: Picking a great spot with a VCR that doesn't work.

Meredith: Lucky you got a VCR...I had to take the laptop to watch a DVD...

Megan: At least you knew it was going to work.

Meredith: True...true. Having sandwich police.

Megan: What were the sandwich police?

Meredith: They had this lady who came around with sandwiches, crackers and ordinary cheese and weak tea, but it was only for the cancer patients. So even though John had taken a couple of days off of work each time I had my treatment and came to sit with me for hours, he wasn't allowed to have sandwiches.

Megan: They never brought us a sandwich. Never did a lady with a cart come around with a sandwich.

            Did she wear candy stripes?

Meredith: No. We don't have candy stripers in Australia. I know what they are thanks to my superior American education. I would like to see a candy striper some day. In real life, as opposed to on TV. She wouldn't give John anything to eat. So I would say, "I will have this, this and this." And then gave it to John. In the end we sent out for pizza.

Megan: In the chemo ward? Do they deliver there?

Meredith: Not to the ward itself. Suzanne actually went downstairs to get it.

            That was the Taxol. That was when we were there all day. It was heavy duty.

And with Taxol you are there for 8 hours pretty much by the time you got stuffed around. It got to the end and I'm looking at the drip and I know the drip is finished. Do you think I can get someone to come and get rid of the goddamn thing? And so in the end I managed to catch the eye of one of them. She said, "Who was your nurse? I said, "I think it was so and so." She said, "I think she's actually left." And she actually ran around saying, "Who's looking after chair number 3?" I know I have actually at this point in my life become chair number 3.

You are no longer an individual. You are chair number 3. And it was beyond her capability to come and change the drip to flush the thing through.

Megan: We had that too. Shannon was pretty aggressive about flipping mine over. You know you get to the end and you still have to shoot through all that saline. So she would just flip it over because she couldn't bear to wait for the nurse to come and do it.

The question was always, "Are you sure it's saline?" Goodness knows what they have in there. It could be anything from the looks of it.

Meredith: You know how when the anti-nausea drugs go in sometimes it gives you a splitting headache? One day that started up really badly for me and Suzanne chased down one of the nurses to ask for some painkillers for me.

The nurse snapped back, "Well she wouldn't have a headache if you weren't all laughing so hard!"

Megan: At least you were having a good time!

Meredith: Of course that just made us laugh harder!

Megan: I sent my little helpers out to get my foods to eliminate. After my first session, I had a cookie accidentally. I didn't know any better. Whole Foods made the best vegan chocolate cookies. It was my comfort food of choice after I got diagnosed. So, I ate one during treatment the first time. And then...

Meredith: ...you can never eat them again.

Megan: Yeah...weeks later I realized wow, I no longer want to eat cookies that have been this huge draw for years. So I started playing with it. Every session, I ate something different.

After the first session I had this huge ice cream craving. And I started eating ice by the case. I eventually decided that was really out of control. So I ate ice cream all through the next session and after I got home that night. That took care of that obsession - forever.

Meredith: I actually was feeling nauseous and the only thing that made me feel better...it was like morning sickness when you are pregnant...the only stuff that would make me feel better was savory stuff. So I had a craving for tomatoes. Fabulous. Let's have really acidic tomatoes when you've just had this drug that is going to attack the lining of your mouth.

OW! Fast track way to having mouth ulcers.

Megan: Did it hurt while you were eating it or after?

Meredith: It was actually after. Actually that sort of accelerated the whole mouth ulcer thing. So I was sucking on a lot of ice for a while. There was kind of this theory that when you were having chemo that if you sucked ice and reduced blood flow to the mouth you don't get them as bad.

Megan: I got mouth ulcers the first time around. They were horrible. But they have this stuff called the Stanford mouth wash. Stanford had come up with a mouth wash specific for chemo mouth ulcers.

They gave it to me and you just kind of swish it around a few times a day, and it got rid of them immediately.

Then they adjusted my dosage the next time around and I never got them again.

Meredith: And they actually got your dosage right.

Megan: Yeah. Exactly. God knows that first time what they actually gave me. That double

dosage. After that we did our own calcu-
lations and wouldn't let them start the
drip until they proved to us that they
weren't double dosing me.

Meredith: Good for you. It makes you realize what
women go through in that situation who
don't have someone to be an advocate
for them.

As I was saying the other night, the question you really need to ask is what your
survival rates are. You don't really want to
ask. As assertive a person as I   am, it
took me half an hour to actually work
myself up to doing that. There was really
so much I couldn't bring myself to deal with.

Megan: Assertive as you may be, it doesn't work
when you're the victim, or whatever you
want to call it.

Meredith: That's all another area of losing control
over it all.

Megan: I had to have my blood drawn and tested
before each chemo treatment. There was
this one person who I always seemed to
get. She was fast, but she left my arm
horribly bruised a couple of times.

Finally, when I got her a third time in a
row, I decided to say something. I told
her that I'd been bruised last time. She
immediately slowed down and became
very concerned and said, "That's not OK!
Who did that to you?" I said, "You did."
She was as gentle as can be after that.

Chemo:
Live Conversation - California, October 2003

Meredith: Until the last time I had chemo, I never actually got sick. And I don't recall ever feeling particularly nauseous. I just felt kind of weird. Just the combination of drugs and stress I guess.

I know I'm glad I never had to drive home from chemo because I always felt really spacey afterwards.

I hated chemo with a passion. The amount of psyching up it took every time to go into that f***ing room. To get up out of bed that morning knowing you had to go and have chemo.

Consciously thinking and counting down the number of times to go. And knowing that was the last shot of that particular round of chemo and then I'd get a break.

I think a lot of getting sick that last time was psychological.

Megan: The worst part for me of going was knowing that I was sentencing myself to a week of feeling like crap.

Sitting there for the treatment was bad enough, but you know you were going to feel worse and worse for a week, and then it would take a couple of weeks to feel halfway normal.

To intentionally subject myself to that was really hard.

And that really affected my diet. I thought, "I'm paying these people to put this poison into my bloodstream. Who the hell cares what I eat? How could that possibly affect me?"

You are getting these really hard core drugs injected in your veins and the nurses are wearing these big protective rubber gloves. It makes you wonder.

Meredith: I know! My nurses wore 2 sets of surgical gloves and goggles. And I'm thinking, "OK, you have to put two layers of gloves on your hands and wear protective glasses to protect yourself from something you are putting directly into my veins."

Megan: And they're watching to make sure your vein doesn't explode in the moment - it was awful.

I didn't really see how diet could do anything then to make a difference.

Meredith: You know we're talking about how you know you're going in there, and you know how bad you're going to feel afterwards. I kept going to the gym and I was very conscious of how debilitating it actually was. I always gave myself a couple of days off after a shot of chemo to give my veins a break before I started heaving weights.

I still managed to go to the gym a couple of times a week, and every week I went in there, I was worse than I had been before.

The aerobic stuff was a nightmare, and instead of actually putting on higher weights I had to decrease weights and reps every time.

And I lost my hair in the gym - that's where I first noticed it falling out.

Megan: Oh my God...

Meredith: That was pretty freaky.

Megan: Why did you keep going to the gym?

Meredith: I actually had been going to the gym for years. At Uni I had lots of free time since I did an arts degree, and I was pretty hard core about my sailing at the time. I was contemplating an Olympic campaign and wanted to work on my strength and endurance.

I started that then and kept it going. The last few years at work were fairly stressful and I found it a good coping mechanism - going a couple of times a week.

I'd pretty well been doing it much of my adult life and had been doing it at the time I got sick.

So I had my surgery and afterwards I got all these brochures with helpful exercises to get your shoulder moving. I couldn't do it - my shoulder was locked.

It got worse, even though I was doing these stretches and I thought something wasn't right. At the same time I had the whole lymphedema discussion with the staff at the hospital so we started looking around for a physio.

So when I went to see her it was ostensibly about working out a way to deal with lymphedema and be able to keep sailing, and then, "Oh by the way, this shoulder doesn't move."

She worked on fixing that first and part of that with her is that there is always an exercise program to go with it. Plus her view on lymphedema was that if you exercised and moved your arm around you were less likely to have a problem.

They had a gym there and you get a discount if you're a client - or a lifetime project as I seem to be turning into for her.

She worked out this program and I started before I started chemo. I remember she wanted to try to get in as much as she could before it began.

The program was about getting my shoulder moving, and general fitness and I always liked weight training.

Megan: I was really lucky. I didn't have any obvious problems with my arm and shoulder after the surgery other than the usual pain, numbness and itchiness. It never would have occurred to me to go see a physical therapist to help with a full recovery.

I happened to have a chiropractor who is also a physical therapist and healer. I went in for a regular appointment after my surgery and she asked how my arm was. I thought it was pretty good, but she worked on it over the next couple of months, and my range of motion and flexibility improved dramatically.

I can't imagine trying to recover fully from such a major surgery without the specific expertise of a physical therapist.

Email From Megan, August 2002

Dear Friends,

I had my first chemo treatment on July 25. I practiced my calming, healing visualizations before and during. Even so, I was pretty anxious about the whole thing. The actual treatment was somewhat anti-climactic. They hooked me up to an I.V. and pumped in anti-nausea medication for 5 minutes, then some saline, then the nurse injects a very red drug directly into the I.V. They like to monitor you as it goes in to make sure you don't have some kind of bad reaction. The worst part is that the drug is refrigerated, so my vein is chilled as it goes in. Then the second chemo drug is dripped in over the course of an hour. The whole process is supposed to take an hour and a half, but it seems to take 2 1/2 - 3 hours.

I was sent home with several prescriptions, and felt fine in the evening. Until they called to tell me they had somehow made an error with my treatment and had only given me half the prescribed dose. I had to go back the next day and do it all over again. I lost it emotionally, yet I was very grateful that they had given me too little rather than too much.
I'll get a total of four treatments (not counting the error induced bonus session), one treatment every

three weeks, as long as my immune system cooperates. I should finish up mid-September. Overall, I feel really good. My energy comes and goes. I can do pretty much anything, but if I overdo it, I pay for it with a day of lying around doing nothing. It sounds good, but forced rest due to fatigue seems to be the most damaging side effect on my emotional state. Otherwise, the only side effects of note are some pretty awful mouth sores which have curtailed my eating (a good thing perhaps) and hair loss.

My hair started coming out in handfuls Thursday. I knew it was coming, but it is a bizarre experience nonetheless. We did the only logical thing - we threw an impromptu head shaving party. Mom and Shannon and Iman came over immediately after receiving my 911 calls. We had a glass of wine and they each (except Iman) took a turn shaving my head. Our dog Elliott was glad his clippers were being turned on me for once.

Now I've had 1/4" stubble all over my head for two days. Probably as soon as I get used to it, the rest will fall out - along with ALL other hair. I'm thinking of drawing in my eyebrows with a magic marker so I only have to do it once.

I went for my first run in a while this week. Other than huffing and puffing, it felt great. I'm still shooting to compete in a triathlon in Sydney in November, although I've shifted my focus from the Olympic distance (about three hours for me to complete) to the Sprint (about 1hr 45 min). Sharon and I are also preparing to compete in the sailing event.

Email From Megan October 2002

Dear Friends -

Let me start by saying no news is good news in this case. I am doing great! My "treatments" are done and the doctors have pronounced me cured!!!

I had my last chemo on September 30. I have to admit I was really dreading it. I had a tough time being positive. Actually, I gave up trying and was depressed and cranky. I just did not want to go through it again. From that upbeat frame of mind, I was pretty sick that last round. It only lasted a week, but I was miserable. Perhaps the drugs do have a cumulative effect.

It feels great to be on the other side. I ran the Susan G. Komen Race for the Cure in San Francisco Sunday. I managed 12 minute miles for the 5K race. I didn't win, but I was thrilled to have participated. There were so many amazing people there. I generally hate drawing attention to myself, but I made an exception and wore the pink "survivor" shirt they gave me and had some cool temporary tattoos on my still bald head. Needless to say, I stood out a bit, which allowed me to talk to some great people.

I spent a lot of time with my niece Iman over the last couple of months. She turned two last week and has been a lifesaver for me. She kept me playing and singing and dancing. We shared the joy and excitement of learning and of practicing until you get it - sometimes trying hundreds of times, not just once or twice. She comforted me when I was sick and pushed me to move when I was just sad. My other adorable niece Madison also had a birthday last week (she is one year old), and we had some great birthday celebrations.

I'm still processing the last five months - trying to understand what it all means, how I'll use the experience, where I want/need to continue growing. The doctor says it will be four months before I feel normal and energetic again. I'm pretty much going 100% now, so it should be really exciting to keep gaining energy for the next few months.

Losing Your Hair

People grow through experience if they
meet life honestly and courageously.
This is how character is built.

ELEANOR ROOSEVELT

Losing your hair is such a part of the breast cancer
experience. It doesn't happen to everyone, but I
suspect everyone goes through the fear of losing it.
Until you lose your hair, you have no idea how important
it is to you. It really affects how we look, the image
we are trying to portray, and how we feel about ourselves.
It is tough to feel beautiful and attractive with a cue
ball head.

The actual process of anticipating the hair loss,
losing the hair, and the miraculous and tedious
return of the hair is a remarkable journey with lots
of opportunities for fun and agony...

Hair:
Live Conversation - California, October 2003

Meredith: I remember when my oncologist told me
about chemo. He said your hair will fall
out two weeks to the day after your first
dose. I don't know about you, but within
about a week every morning when I woke
up I was checking the pillow to see if it
had started.

And thinking, "Is that how much hair you normally lose when you're sleeping, or is it going now? When's it going to happen?" And being kind of hyper sensitive to that.

It got to two weeks to the day and I didn't notice anything particularly that morning or in the shower, which you know is when you usually notice, and trotted off to the gym.

I did my warm up and I was actually doing my stretches lying on a towel on the rubber mat and sat up, looked down and thought, "Oh, shit." There really shouldn't be that much hair there if you've just been laying down for a minute.

I thought, "Well, that's it." And I ran my hand through my hair and came out with a handful so...I finished the gym work out anyway.

Megan: Of course!

Meredith: Of course. Then I got home and rang my hairdresser and said, "Look, this is the situation, can I get in today because I really need it all chopped off?" She was a bit shocked and taken aback and said, "Sure, come over whenever you want."

I rang Suzanne to say, "It's going!" So she met me over there at my hair dresser.

Meredith: My hair was longer than I have now. I always had a thing about big ears, so even though my hair got progressively shorter as I got older, it always covered my ears. I got over that after 10 months with no hair.

It was funny because I was sitting there and Suzanne said, "You're not losing your hair!" So I ran my hand through my hair to show her and she said, "Ah..."

So we had a glass of wine and Deanne gave me the number one cut all the way over. And I had my baseball cap with me because my sisters down south had been buying designer caps for me.

I was pretty pumped and psyched and ready, and she shaved it all off and I thought, "Well, that's not too bad." Because I still had eyebrows at that stage.

Megan: Yeah, it makes a difference.

Meredith: I was in that heightened state you are at the beginning thinking, "Big deal, it's only a couple of months, I can deal with this."

Megan: It's not really going to affect my life...

Meredith: Not realizing...because you don't. How could you possibly realize the impact on how people react to you?

Megan: Why would you want to?

Meredith: You just don't see it.

I'd rung John and told him that was the deal, my hair is going to be gone by the time you get home. He came home and went to get Dexter, and Dex was just a hoot.

We'd pre-warned him and he was in fits of laughter - kind of cool. Kept running his hand over my head giggling, saying, "Oh God, oh God."

I remember reading that at any time only one third of the hair on your head is growing and that's what you lose. And it keeps growing in between, so in the next two weeks after you lose it, more starts to grow back and then you lose it again.

Usually in the shower - I remember having to hose down the shower curtain every time it started going again - bits of hair going everywhere.

I always had a baseball cap full of bits of hair that kept falling out - pretty gross.

Megan: I never let mine grow back after we shaved it.

Meredith: You kept shaving it off? I got a "number one" buzz cut all the way over and then just let it do its thing. I got it trimmed up when it started to grow back during radiation.

And it wasn't bad after three months of growing back before I started the second lot of chemo.

What was weird the second time was that I hadn't had the chance to get my head shaved so it all came out in the shower. I checked into the hotel in San Francisco, went up and had a shower and lost it down the drain.

And what was odd was that because you don't lose it all at once I had these odd stray hairs that were about an inch long left so I had to go out and get it shaved.

Straight after I went down and asked the concierge where I could get a hair cut, and there was a little salon across the road - they were really wigged out.

I said, "Look, here's the deal, I had chemo and all I want is for you to run a clipper over it." The guy there was really wigged out, but eventually he got with the program and chopped it off.

And it cost me ten bucks, which was pretty ridiculous considering what was involved. Particularly since my hair dresser at home - she was really cool and kept doing my hair for free for months during treatment and just afterwards. Until I said, "OK - time to colour it now because I'm not keeping it grey!"

So I never actually shaved it, just used the clippers on the shortest setting - what we call a "number one".

Megan: And then you'd go with whatever came back in?

Meredith: I think I got it trimmed up a couple of times during chemo because there were still the little bits coming back in, and I was still trying to pull it off as an intentional hairstyle.

Megan: Yeah...it gets a little thin for that...

Meredith: And then my eyebrows started to go and it was even harder to pull off.

             I went in to see my surgeon for one check up, and I'd gone and bought a pair of Doc Martens - going the full butch route at that stage.

He laughed and said he had another young woman who was a patient who'd done the same thing, but she'd also actually got her head tattooed. Can you imagine - you remember how sensitive your scalp was - and she got it tattooed! I don't know how she went through with that.

My oncologist told me before I started chemo that my hair would come back dark and curly so when I saw him it was like, "Hello?????? Curly and grey????"

Megan: Mine came back greyer for sure.

Meredith: Well why wouldn't it with the amount of stress we went through.

The eyebrows were the tough thing though, they go progressively. I do have a clear recollection in San Francisco that time my hair fell out that my eyebrows had started to come back during radiation so it actually looked kind of cool.

I could pull it off to some extent as a butch hair cut if I had good eyebrows. By the time I finished the second lot of chemo I could actually count the ones left.

And not only my eyebrows, I lost my eyelashes.

Megan: Oh my God.

Meredith: That sucked. I had about three left on one side and a few on the other. Which led to some compulsive attempts with make-up.

Megan: You can't do anything with three eye lashes!!!

Meredith: You try, baby, you try! I got to the drawing on eyebrows stage because that was too weird not having eyebrows. I liked your suggestion of using a Sharpie to draw them on!

Megan: That would be my plan, but you know I had so much to start with that I could lose 90% and look pretty good...

Meredith: You had much better eyebrows than I ever had through the whole process.

My eyebrows have never come quite back to where they were.

So I got to the stage of drawing on eye brows, and made some attempts with mascara because no eyelashes is an even worse look.

People's reactions were interesting. I either got people who were scared because of the butch look and ran away, or those who knew it was chemo hair and chased after me with their story.

My birthday was in the middle of my second lot of chemo and I was really feeling like crap. Julie and Jules decided to come up and cheer me up, and Jules actually got up here before Julie did.

We were sitting around talking and Jules announced that she had come up with the perfect thing to do for my birthday - that she was going to get her head shaved with me.

So we trooped off to my hairdresser and explained the situation to her, and she gave Jules the number one all the way over, and then we had to go pick Julie up from the airport.

The look on Julie's face when she got off the plane to find these two bald-headed butch women waiting - it was like, "I can never leave you two alone!"

Megan: Well she had a point!

Meredith: That was really sweet of Jules to do that and she also came and sat through chemo with me - it was one of those all day marathons, which was really sweet too.

So walking around there would be people who would spot me as having chemo hair and would chase me down. Once we went to do the grocery shopping and I got tired and sat down in the mall outside the supermarket to wait for John.

I actually had Dexter with me at the time, and this insensitive man came charging up and said, "Have you got cancer?", and, "Is it breast cancer?" Then he went into this long story about his wife and her treatment.

I'm sitting in a f***ing shopping mall for God's sake, and not wanting to talk about any of this, and to have a stranger come up and front you up. In front of Dexter too.

I never really went bald much in public - always wore the baseball cap.

I wore a cap for the first few weeks back at work too. In the end I just couldn't be bothered with it and decided they'd just have to put up with me bald. It was really a conscious effort to walk around like that.

I don't know why it's so hard - I mean everyone I worked with knew anyway. I wasn't really comfortable with walking around looking like crap. That was tough.

Megan: Well you know both of us went through this in this state of denial with, "It's not really going to affect me and it's not going to slow me down." But when your hair falls out...

You can pretend like you're not sick and if someone comes over you can prop yourself up and not feel great but fight your way through it, but you can't hide not having any hair.

I remember I went to this support group before I started treatment, right after I was diagnosed. There were all these people and I could tell right away who was wearing a wig and who wasn't.

There was this really young woman - she was younger than I was - wearing this wig. I was horrified. I did not want people to ever look at me and say, "That is obviously a wig."

Meredith: Like, why do we have to have bad hair too?

Megan: It was so obviously a wig. I remember talking to her about where she got her wig, and she told us she had a friend of her's who just decided to go around bald.

That was the first time that even occurred to me. I thought, "Wow, how courageous. How amazing that you would just decide to be bald." That kind of planted the seed for me.

But I was really not at all going to go that route.

Meredith: I just decided up front, nope, not going to do a wig.

It's not going to be me, I'm not going to find a wig with a hair style that I would consider and people are going to tell anyway and I would rather just...not do it.

Megan: Because I worked in sales I pretty much thought I needed a wig and I didn't have any clue what that experience was going to be like.

I remember kind of scoping out things long before I lost my hair. You know, looking in windows, but there was no way in hell I was going through the door.

It felt like something I just had to do. I was in sales and I had to deal with clients. I thought had to have a wig, but was freaked out about actually doing it.

I remember one day I grabbed Mom. We'd been doing something else and it didn't fit in the schedule but I said,

"Here's a wig shop, and my hair's going to be gone in a week."

I did not want to be in a position of, "My hair's coming out and now I need a wig." I wanted one off the shelf. So we went in and we spent an hour. You know I hate to shop for clothing and I don't wear make up - I hate all of that, so I said to Mom, "You just need to pick a wig for me".

It wasn't a particularly great shop, and they didn't have a particularly good selection. We picked one that kind of worked. We could have gotten it styled in addition.

I remember we had a big family function that weekend. I went and I still had hair - it hadn't started coming out yet. I took the wig, and was modeling it, and the feedback was...marginal.

It looked like a f***ing wig. People were like, "Well maybe you could get a more updated hair style." And I said, "Well I bought it last week."

Meredith: The time that Jules came in with me for chemo we were sitting there and going through all the brochures in the ward.

There was one particularly appalling one from a wig manufacturer and it was truly hilarious. Our favourite was from the men's wigs, and they had a mullet. An ash blonde/grey mullet.

And each wig had a name, and this one was called the "Kevin". Now there is not a less cool name you could have in Australia than a "Kevin".

Can you imagine? "Yes, I want a Kevin! I want an '80s ash blonde mullet wig called a Kevin!"

Megan: That's hilarious!

We'd been to see my great-aunt in Illinois that summer, right after my surgery. She wears wigs all the time.

She wears them in the winter time to keep her head warm. She has a pretty good head of hair, but she puts on these little wigs. And she gets all of these magazines for mail order wigs. We had the best time looking through the catalogs laughing about which one might work for me.

They were about $40 a wig, which was really cheap. But, I was definitely concerned about having a mail order wig. That really worried me.

And they have lame names too, like "Sarah". So I'm looking at them and thinking, "I just can't trust the picture of the Sarah, or that particular color." It just didn't seem right.
So we went into the shop and instead of a $40 mail order wig I got a $150 crap wig with fake hair.

Meredith: What did you do with it?

Megan: Well I bought the little stand, so it sat on its little stand in the bedroom, really looking like $150. My oncologist was more than happy to write me a prescription for my "cranial prosthesis" which should have been reimbursable from my insurance. Apparently only reimbursable if you go to the right store, which I didn't know.

It was a complete waste of money, which upset me. And, I found out you can't return a wig. I eventually sold it at a garage sale for $5.

Not long after buying the wig, I don't know what I was doing that day, but I remember coming home and noticing my hair was coming out, just like you said, in a way it's not supposed to.

My hair was shoulder length - it seems really long now, although it wasn't long hair. And when you've got handfuls of hair that's eight inches long, that's really long.

I knew in a couple of hours that it was going to take weeks - it felt like it was going to take forever - to actually all fall out, and I couldn't deal with it at that rate.

So I called my Mom and my sister. They came over and we had a glass of wine and we played with the clippers. And I have all these pictures of my hair in these kind of screwball pieces.

I ended up with something that was about an inch long, like a little buzz cut, and it was a good transitional piece. It was kind of falling out over the next two weeks. It didn't go down to nothing like I thought it would.

Meredith: It seems like that when you run your hands through your hair and it comes out in handfuls. It's weird and it's messy.

Megan: Yep, the mess is awful, and every time it happens it's a reminder of being sick, and it's really depressing - to have a handful of hair.

Meredith: And it keeps happening, two weeks after every time you have chemo. You wake up in the morning and there's hair all over your pillow, coming off in the shower and all over your clothes.

Megan: It's like a symbol of being sick, and what could be more dramatic than losing your hair?

Meredith: It's something you can't cover up. You can cover up the fact you've had surgery, but not your hair. And that's where people focus, on your face.

Megan: I had my little one inch buzz cut - maybe it was even shorter than that. It was less than an inch but it still looked like I had hair. So I went water skiing. I had permission from my surgeon and oncologist!

It made perfect sense to me that if I could hold the rope and do it, why not.

So we'd been out on the water all day and my experience of being in the water was, every time I got in and out I had to put sunscreen on my head, because the hair was thin. I had, I don't know, a half, two thirds of my hair. It was thin and you could see my scalp.

I was worried about having this fried head, so I put sunscreen on and I'd have this handful of hair, and it made me sick. I'd get out of the water and have handfuls of crappy hair in my hand and it was really depressing and just awful and I didn't want to deal with it.

I could have gone on for days, but I didn't want to do it. So when we got back to the dock it was early afternoon and the sun was going down, and I said to Sharon, "I can't deal with this. Would you shave it off?"

So we were in the middle of nowhere, really hours from anything decent and she had a little, one blade crap razor. We sat down and she starts shaving my head with a little bar of soap and a little bucket of water. It took a long time be cause she's - you know Sharon - she's trying to get a perfectly smooth head - and she's going over four or five times.

Finally I just said, "Please don't go over it four times because I'm getting a little razor burn on my head."

Our friend came over and said, "Do you need a glass of wine?" And it was perfect, because damn straight I did. We sat there and had a glass of wine, and she talked to me about other stuff and I was completely distracted. I alternated between bawling and laughing.

It was like a symbol of not being whole, of not being OK. We were on our deck during this, and an eight year old girl from the cabin next door came past and said, "What are you doing?"

Sharon said, "Oh, she's sick and having medicine..." And you know I didn't want that to have to be my identity. Here's this sick person, and that's why she looks like this.

I got through the shaving part and I was able to put sunscreen on and water ski, so I felt healthy and able to do stuff I wanted to do.

I think I wore my wig a total of 5 times. Every time was for a client meeting.

I remember one very clearly. It was a new client who had been referred to me. It was a multi-million dollar house with a lot of complications, so I asked a very experienced agent to go with me to meet the client.

When we got there, this woman had forgotten we had an appointment. She recovered enough to give us a tour of the house. As we were walking through the kitchen, she picks up a bottle of olive oil, dumps some in her hands and puts it through her hair. She had really curly hair, and she said that was what tamed her hair!

Meredith: OH MY GOD!

Megan: It was bizarre! It was a business meeting even if it was in her house, and she's putting olive oil in her hair.

It was one of my first public appearances in my wig, so I was really self conscious. And it was mid-July and really hot. The day before when I'd gone to meet with this woman I'd just had my little stubble head, right, so the next day I put on the wig and feel like a complete idiot.

And she's like, "Oh, I didn't recognize you." I'm thinking, "I don't know who the hell I am anyway, so don't worry about it."

As soon as we left, after two hours of sweating and olive oil and bizarre meetings I said, "I hope you don't mind but I've got to take this wig off.", and I threw it on the floor.

It was really a relief to have it off. It was hot and it was uncomfortable and it was not at all me.

Meredith: I think work-wise, you had it harder than me. I could manage things so I didn't have to put on a public face and go out. I used to do a lot of public speaking but once I lost my hair I pulled back from that.

I didn't do any really proactive stuff, going out and looking for sponsorship. I did most of that by phone and email.

When I was really bald and had to meet with people I just wore a baseball cap.

Megan: But that doesn't really hide it...

Meredith: Yeah, but it made me feel better about myself.

I did have to speak at a breakfast function in Sydney once. A high powered, business women's breakfast with 200 movers and shakers in all industries. That was really tough to get up and do. No baseball cap that time.

Megan: The funny thing is I normally wore base ball caps all the time before being sick. That was my identity. And being bald with a baseball cap just didn't work - it still looks odd.

Meredith: When I lost my hair in San Francisco I had to spend a week going around meeting with the presidents of different foundations, traveling with a group of other professionals.

I had my baseball caps but they didn't really work with the suit. So we got in on a weekend and I said to my boss, "I don't know about this - you know what I really need - I need a fedora."

I needed a cool hat, to go with my cool suits. So I researched the phone directories and found this really cool hat shop. We went there and I bought two really cool fedoras - he bought one too so we were the Bobsy twins.

So I spent the week running around in my fedora and my suit to all of my meetings - I'm hoping they just thought I was eccentric.

Megan: It was probably a really good look!

Meredith: It was better than the baseball cap and I figured it was better than the bald look.

One of the other people there said to my boss, "Why doesn't she just wear a wig?" and he laughed and said, "She is so not a wig girl!"

My favorite work story from that period is that my Queensland manager had a business contact that he thought would assist with our fundraising in that state and he wanted me to meet with him.

We went to the meeting and this was while I was having radiation and had a bit of hair grown back and I'd had it trimmed around the edges so it just looked like a really butch hair cut. Maybe half a centimeter long.

I'm sitting there talking to this guy and he starts talking about his motivations in wanting to get involved. He told me he used to do a lot of work for a cancer organization but decided to move on because, "Let's face it, when people get cancer, they just die, its just too depressing to hang around."

Megan: Oh my God.

Meredith: And my Queensland manager was just sitting there looking stricken, like Bambi in my headlights. I just burst out laughing and said, "Look I just think I ought to just explain to you that the haircut isn't just a fashion statement, I've actually just recovered from chemo."

He was then equally stricken, and I think it was great emotional blackmail because he was pretty much committed to the cause from then on having made the ultimate faux pas.

Mind you, I was actually pleased about the fact that he had not just assumed I was sick.

My Victorian fundraising manager, who was just a sweetheart, met with me in Melbourne around that time and honestly thought my hair looked fantastic that short.

And other people - even John said to me, "Are you going to keep it that short?" But it was just too confronting and too close to where I'd been.

I think at the time I was just thinking, "Well this is just one of those things and I've just got to get through it." But it ain't fun.

Megan: Well I had some breakthroughs with it really. I had to come to terms with this is who I am. To be able to march around and not have to hide under that wig was a huge piece. I talked to my therapist about it a few times because it was not an easy decision.

The biggest challenge for me was to show up in my office with no hair. I shouldn't have cared what people I don't really know think. But it was important to me. Walking into my office when I had only worked there for a few months was difficult for me.

It was more than wanting to look good. I know good hair is a bigger issue for you.

If I walk around with bad hair, I generally don't care. But to walk in with a bald head was a symbol of I'm sick, and now I have to talk about being sick. I had to deal with feeling and looking sick and weak.

Meredith: I think that's really the sort of crux of it for me, although I have a bigger fixation with good hair. It was the bit about being obviously sick and not wanting that to be your identity and for people to bring it up and relate to you that way.

Megan: And I knew that I didn't want people to see me and think, "Oh you're sick you obviously can't do your job." It was really terrifying to me.

By the time I got to the Gay Games I didn't really care as much. I had finished chemo, and I had a bald head. But I'd been bald for months. My experience was more like, "What's the big deal?"

And it was hilarious because people had no clue, people on my own team didn't even know.

Meredith: The Aussies just thought you were doing the butch thing.

Megan: I can't even believe that...

Meredith: I was saying, "I...don't...think...so...that's chemo hair."

Megan: Now when I look back, I know I looked like hell.

Meredith: Well it's the pale thing - you looked pale, with dark shadows under your eyes. I looked worse because I'd been through it twice - you didn't have as bad circles under your eyes. But we were both really pale.

Megan: Yeah, that's what I saw when I looked at that video.

But having met me for the first time, you wouldn't have known that. I didn't look that bad. Well you knew, but...

Meredith: Only because of my personal experience.

Megan: Yeah, I looked really sick. And you know I was looking at that triathlon video, and I don't know if I could do it now but there was some huge determination.

There was no way I was not going to do that. I'd been thinking about that for too long, it was really important to me. I just kind of ploughed through it.

Meredith: And then demoralized people by beating them.

Megan: Yeah, well, they didn't know.

Meredith: Until they read about it in the paper.

Megan: That was pretty cool. And you know I drank that whole trip and we just had a great time. We didn't really slow down. Although, I did have to go to bed early.

Meredith: You did crash early. The night we met you left early.

Megan: Well the sailing was really hard on me. So we'd have a drink and a bath and then I was asleep by 8 or 9 o'clock. That was my experience.

And we didn't do anything other than sail, and get my bike, and do the triathlon. We didn't go to any other events.

Meredith: It takes a long while to get that back. Two years afterwards I was still crashing early.

Megan: Well that makes me feel better, because it's only been a year for me and I don't think I'm at my best. I can't believe it's only what I eat and how I exercise... there has to be some other factor.

Meredith: What was done to us, all those drugs. When I talked to my surgeon at one of my annual checkups about the fatigue told me his sister is now 6 or 7 years out from treatment and she still suffers from the fatigue.

It's depressing.

Megan: Yeah, it really makes me angry. It's one thing to age. Aging is bad enough, but then you've got to deal with this crap.

Lymphedema

You were once wild here. Don't let them tame you!

ISADORA DUNCAN

Megan's Thoughts 12/27/03:

I've been really lucky. I haven't had any symptoms of lymphedema - knock on wood!! That doesn't mean I haven't worried about it.

I remember going to visit my great aunt in Illinois as a kid. She was in her 70's, and on the heavy side. And one of her arms was three times the size of the other. It was huge. It looked really uncomfortable and not very functional.

I remember being told she had lymphedema, which meant nothing to me except it was something I never wanted to have. And I also remember hearing that she had breast cancer many years ago, when they cut away half your chest as standard treatment.

When I was diagnosed, I thought about my great aunt and couldn't help but worry a little about lymphedema. I tried to ignore all references to it, yet was drawn to some of the pamphlets out of curiosity. Was I at risk? What causes it? How could I avoid it?

I found a lot of mixed messages, and the huge list of things recommended in order to minimize risk sounded a lot like giving up on life - no hot tubs or flying or upper body activities like swimming or kayaking or pushups.

I decided the best approach for me was to avoid worrying about it. And since they don't know exactly what really causes it, I thought I'd go on with my fully active life and assume I would be fine.

That approach has worked for the most part, but the concern still follows me around, somewhere in the back of my mind.

From: Megan
Sent: Saturday, February 01, 2003

I'm curious, did they take all of your lymph nodes? I got the lymphedema chat, but more in a "nothing to be concerned with" context (at least that is what I chose to hear).

I met a woman in Las Vegas in December, a couple of months after chemo, who zoned in on me thanks to my signature hairdo as it was just coming back. She developed lymphedema two years after surgery while mixing cookie dough. Not exactly the conversation I wanted to have while standing in line for a show in Las Vegas.

I dismissed her story as not relevant to me because of the age difference (she was in her 60's) and I've already done everything you are not supposed to do.

From: Meredith
Sent: Saturday, February 01, 2003

Let's see now, lymphedema stuff. They took about 10 I think and my surgeon said he thought they left plenty behind, but lymph stuff can be funny - they don't really know how it all works and there was the possibility I could have problems.

The very comforting brochure they gave me in the hospital had a list of things you had to stop doing like not getting sun burnt, not carrying any pressure on that arm, not getting any bruises or injuries on that arm and so on. All of which is pretty par for the course in sailing.

My physio's view was that the only thing that moves lymph around your system is using your muscles, and the more I worked my arm the better it would be. She figured if I didn't get it after two years we'd have it licked, and she appears to be right. Although I think I need to keep the gym program up because my shoulder starts to go stiff again when I slack off.

The only problem I have is flying - when I flew to the States when I was having chemo my arm and hand swelled up over the flight and it was pretty uncomfortable for a week or so before going down. Given the amount of traveling I do I ended up getting one of those full elastic sleeves made up - incredibly uncomfortable on the flight, but at least my arm stays its normal size.

It makes me look like an escaped burn victim and I keep hoping someone will take pity on me and upgrade me to business class, but it hasn't happened yet!

I am assuming since you didn't mention it you haven't had any problems - good for you!

Lymphedema:
Live Conversation - Las Vegas, October 2003

Meredith: During my last check up debacle, I had to wait four days to get the results. So I started renovating the kitchen - which I had been planning to do that weekend, but I got quite manic about it.

Doing the kitchen was something I'd been wanting to do for some time and it involved lots of my favourite activities - ripping things apart, building things, getting to use power tools and saws and nails and hammers, and getting to create things.

I've restored a sailing boat every winter for the last couple of years and I didn't have one of those projects this year so this was my replacement.

John was sailing that weekend which was cool because it gave me absolute free reign and control over things. I'd been slowly pulling it apart on Friday, and then John came home that evening and we really got stuck into it.

Then he was sailing all Saturday, and Dexter was off around the house doing his own thing so I was free to keep pulling it to pieces.

I got to about one o'clock in the afternoon and realized that the veins in the back of my left hand were really sore and my left arm and hand had started to swell.

Which was fabulous - not. It really pissed me off at the time, because I'm right handed so its not like it was doing any thing, it was just along for the ride.

I mean, it helped with pulling down things but it wasn't doing any of the sawing or hammering or anything.

And I'm thinking, three years down the track, this should not be a problem. And it swelling up just brings up so many things for me - the whole fear of lymphedema which has been a big issue all along.

Plus the veins hurting in the back of my hand is just what it was like all through chemo.

I was conscious at the time that I knew it was swelling up and I was really pissed off and angry about it because why should this still be happening to me after three years, after all I've done?

So of course I should have stopped working but I didn't because I was too angry about the fact it was happening and I was determined to keep working all the way through.

My sister Stephanie was in town and she and Suzanne dropped over to see the state of the demolition and rebuilding. Suzanne and I were having a chat about waiting to go back and get the results of my check up, and I told her that my hand had started to swell during the day, which I was very annoyed about.

And she said that she had wondered if that was going to happen. Great, so I'm not the only person who thinks about it. I did actually give up for a while then after they left and lay down for an hour or two and waited for it to go down, which was really slow and painful.

So it went down and John came home and was really impressed with what I'd done that day with the kitchen, and I told him that my arm had started to swell during the day.

And he said, "That's OK, I'll do all the sawing and stuff tomorrow." Which was really sweet of him, but I was really pissed off again. Not because I like saw ing - I hate hand sawing hardwood, and I don't have a suitable power tool to do it with. I was angry because of the idea again of a physical limitation.

If I had been in my right mind I would have thought, "Terrific! I don't have to do it!" But that's not what was in my head. The thought I had was, "It's been three years, and I am going to have to keep putting up with this?"

You know once I'd got through the physio and got my shoulder moving and everything I thought the physical stuff for me was over. Physically I was fixed.

The last 12 months has really been about dealing with the emotional and mental side of it. But now this physical limitations stuff keeps popping up again. That's tough.

Work and People

*A positive attitude may not solve all your problems,
but it will annoy enough people to
make it worth the effort.*

HERM ALBRIGHT

Work and People:
Live Conversation - California, June 2003

Meredith: I did try and keep going in and working from the office. But it's a big office. We have a couple of hundred people there. They've all known me for a number of years. And so when I was in my office, trying to work, it was just a continual stream of people coming to my door and wanting to talk about how I was and how it was going.

I wanted to work. Work is the thing that is normal. Back into normality, back into your life. I needed to do something. And you've just got person after person who wants to bring up all this stuff. So that was kind of hard.

And also, to be honest, for a lot of those people, it was all about them. And then they give you the helpful book and it's all about them working out their issues.

You talked about that too, Megan. Where you would have people come up to you and say, "How are you?" And you'd say, "Oh, I'm doing pretty well." You'd give a fairly innocuous answer, maybe give them a little about where you were, and then they'd launch into some 10, 15, 20 minute diatribe telling you some story about someone they knew.

Megan: Right. People I knew, people I didn't particularly know, people I met. And I'm not one to go into my own drama anyway. And so it just didn't take much for them to go on and on. And I think that what happened is I didn't have my strength - to think and to move on. Whatever was going on in my head seemed to be in slow motion. So to be able to walk away or to say, "Uh, huh.",and get out of the conversation. I'm not very good at that to begin with, and then I'd lost all ability to speak up for myself.

I remember getting sucked into conversations, and the obvious, logical thing to do would be to walk away and get out of the conversation and I physically couldn't do it. I physically couldn't get out of the conversation that I didn't want to be in. I had no capacity to do that. And that was really frustrating, especially when I look back on it, I realize that I didn't have any personal power. I just didn't have any power to make a decision or to take any action or to tell somebody to buzz off - even in very nice terms.

Meredith: Everyone suddenly seems to think that whatever they've known about you in the past, like being an analytical introvert, suddenly you've got cancer so you will now be totally emotional and open, and you can emote and you can empathize and you want to talk about this. No. I don't, actually. I don't want to go there. And then there are all these people who come up with their particular cancer cure or their cancer diet.

If you aren't doing it then it is your fault you see. And you know, if you do this then you will suddenly be cured. And if you're not doing this then you are at fault. I don't need that.

Megan: I am still getting it. I was in a personal growth seminar recently. The fact that I'd had cancer did not come up in the course of four full days of people sharing about their lives. Working through some of the issues was one of the motivators for doing the seminar. And it turned out there was other stuff in my life that was more important to me.

And so when it finally came up, every body in the thing was like, "OHHHHH!" Shocked. That I had had it. That it hadn't come up. That I hadn't talked about it. It seems as soon as it comes up, someone is right there, chasing you. So the one that was chasing me recently is really into certain form of medicinal exercises. She cornered me, told me about them and even called me later to follow up.

She talked about this guy and they are shrinking tumors and all this stuff. I said, "I'm OK, the tumor is gone. You know what, I looked at a lot of things and this is what I decided to do for treatment, and you know what, my treatment is over."

Meredith: You did say that?

Megan: Yea I did. And she said, "Well, you don't want it to come back."

Meredith: OHHHHHHH. If you don't do this then you are going to relapse.

Megan: Which is the same thing as it's your fault that it happened in the first place.

Meredith: I attempted to keep sailing. While I was doing that I had John crewing for me and I looked pretty bloody awful. And there was actually one regatta where we barely made it through the last race because I was just too sick to keep going.

And I kept copping grief from this woman at the sailing club. The things this woman put me through because I kept trying to sail.

I couldn't sail in the normal Club races because the Brisbane River is full of nasty bugs.

There was another regatta at Lake Cootharaba, which was open water. I thought I would try and do it. The first conversation with her was, you know when I'm sailing all I wear are board shorts and if it's warm enough, then all I wear under the life jacket is a bikini top because I like to get a tan. And I figured at this stage skin cancer is the least of my worries, right.

So, I have her chasing me around the beach giving me this lecture on how exposure to the sunlight reduces your immunity and hasn't your oncologist talked to you about this. You really should be wearing a balaclava and gloves and a full sleeved top and cap and what-ever else. And I am thinking, "Well, no. As a matter of fact my oncologist told me to do whatever I enjoy and makes me feel good."

And I could not get rid of the woman. And I am thinking, "Go Away! You are not the person treating me."

There I am trying to enjoy myself doing something I like and I have this woman hounding me telling me no sailing.

Megan: My oncologist was great. All the way through, he said, "You do whatever you want to do.", and if I wanted to do triathlons, "Go for it." When I said half way through treatment, "Can I go water skiing?", he said, "Absolutely." It was great. Even now he's like, "Just don't worry about anything. You're fine."

Meredith: You know mine was like that. If you want to go to the States, fine, I'll just give you drugs, and I'll give you a note to give to a doctor if you get sick over there. And he was actually going to be over for a conference. I thought he was going to suggest we catch up over there or something.

He said, "You know I'm going to be over there anyway for a conference anyway and don't worry about it at all."

But you know, other people, other medical professionals weren't so great.

My surgeon was brilliant. My three main professionals, my surgeon, my radiologist and my oncologist were all great. They didn't put any limitations on what I could do. And they were very supportive.

But that wasn't always my experience. One thing that really annoyed me was that is seemed to me that the system - particularly chemo - seemed to be set up according to what worked best for the staff, not the patients.

I told you all my stories about chemo and getting a different nurse each time, most of whom couldn't get the needle in at their first attempt.

There was one fantastic nurse who was just incredibly caring and connected and reassuring and who always got the needle in at her first try.

So we tried everything we could to make sure I got her the next time and no matter what we tried or who we spoke to we could not make it happen.

We found out afterwards that there was a secret policy to never let a patient have the same nurse twice so you didn't get attached to them! How stupid is that! And it obviously didn't work because all it takes is one good experience and you are pretty attached! There is no continuity of care.

I'd spent my whole career working in charities that deliver client-centered services, where things are run according to what your clients want. This seemed like the complete opposite and was a hell of a shock.

Megan: When I went for my last check up, my oncology nurse took me into the chemo treatment room to take my blood pressure rather than the exam room. It was horrible. I don't ever want to be back in that room. Definitely not for something as routine as taking my blood pressure. I honestly don't know what she was thinking, except maybe she is completely desensitized to the whole thing.

Meredith: Maybe they spend so much of their time dealing just in their specific area of the medical stuff, and with so many people coming through that there is no time to really think about how it impacts us at an individual level.

I know that was how I felt on several occasions.

After I got my motorcycle license, a group of health professionals who knew me asked my sister Suzanne, "How's your sister doing?" She said, "Oh great! She just got her motorcycle license!" Their first response was, "Did she ask her medical oncologist about that?" Suzanne said, "Well no she didn't..."

Megan: He'd say "Well, no. I prefer this model of motorcycle."

Meredith: She said, "She's not actually having treatment anymore. Therefore it's irrelevant."

They are the ones that give you the most grief. And so you are dealing with every-thing else and then you have other people's expectations put on top of you.

Support Groups

Just remember, we're all in this alone.

LILY TOMLIN

Support Groups:
Live Conversation - California, October 2003

Megan: As soon as I was diagnosed, we went and
          saw the nurse educator and we spent a
          lot of time with her. I can't remember
          specifically but she must have mentioned
          some support programs, and the surgeon
          passed on some resources as did the
          oncologist, and so they were kind of coming
          from all directions.

          I was kind of on a quest and as soon as
          people heard about my diagnosis, they
          would send me websites and links and
          people to talk to. I actually did call several
          people who had breast cancer who had
          been referred to me by friends of friends,
          basically.

          I ended up with a collection of resources.
          I knew who was offering support groups.
          I knew you were supposed to talk about
          stuff so the support groups seemed like
          the right thing to do.

          I also knew that as an introvert it's very
          uncomfortable for me to go into a group

setting and talk about my stuff. I do much better one on one, or in my head. Although I don't think I actually figured out anything really significant by myself.

I honestly don't remember the chronology of when it happened. It was before my treatment started. It must have been before I started chemo that I went to a support group.

There's a place in Palo Alto that was really helpful - the Community Breast Health Project.

I went and they have all the research studies and all of the stuff that's been published in the medical journals. Any issue that I was concerned about they were able to look up and give me any published material on it. Which was great as it gave me the information I needed to make the decision to go ahead with chemo.

I didn't really want to get kicked into early menopause. That wouldn't have stopped me from the chemo, but it was a concern. So I wanted to know how often that happened.

And then there was somebody else that said that Adriamycin, the red chemo drug, causes heart damage. They definitely won't give it to you twice. If the cancer comes back that version is not available to you. I knew somebody who was a friend of a friend who had chosen to go CMF instead of AC because she was worried about heart damage.

I decided I had a really strong heart to begin with, so if I lost a little tiny piece nobody would notice, and I wasn't super worried about it. But it was kind of in the back of my mind as a concern, I wanted to know how big of an issue it actually is.

So those were the kinds of things we were looking up.

One time when I happened to go, I coincided my visit with a support group evening.

There must have been 6 or 8 women there, and the topic was reconstruction, which I'd already decided not to do. They had a surgeon there to address any questions.

I felt not at all related to any of the people there. To me, they looked really upset and they looked like victims and they just looked incredibly depressed.

I was in my denial phase, thinking, "This is no big deal. This is going to make me stronger." That was my coping strategy at the time. It seemed like a more powerful place to be than, "I'm weak and I'm a victim and I'm going to die."

I don't know what they were really thinking, but to me they seemed stuck and unhappy.

I met one woman at the support group who was 26 and really angry. She was really angry about being that young and having cancer.

Meredith: Well you would be, wouldn't you?

Megan: At the time, having someone that I planned to be with for the rest of my life definitely influenced my decision not to do reconstruction. When I talked to other people who were not with somebody, the prospect of dating was really a big issue.

To have a scar or no breast or a less than perfectly shaped breast is a really big issue.

I don't know how the prospect of dating might have affected my decision, but I wasn't worried about that at all. I don't think it would have changed anything I did, but I would have had a lot more to think about.

This young woman at the support group was just really angry about what she was having to go through at her age. Which I didn't see as particularly powerful or useful either. Although I completely understood where she was coming from, I didn't want to go there.

And it honestly wasn't what I was experiencing at that time. Although, some of it did come up for me later.

So I'm there on a topic that I'm not interested in, I can't believe that they're actually talking about doing these things to their body that would be required in reconstruction.

I didn't like the attitude of the people there where it's either victim or angry, and I didn't feel really connected to any of them.

I stuck it out, and then I didn't really see any need to go back to that group.

The only thing was that I really wanted Sharon to find a support group.

Sharon reacted really badly when I started chemo. We had some extreme upsets going on. I really wanted her to be able to talk to people and so I kept asking her, "What kind of support group would work?"

We couldn't really go to a traditional couples group. Neither one of us had any interest in sitting around with a bunch of married people because we figured that a guy's experience of this would be really different than Sharon's.

I kept calling the local Gay and Lesbian Center. They have had support groups for lesbians with breast cancer in the past and so I eventually got a call and they said, "We're starting one up again."

So it was Sharon and me and these two other women along with a volunteer facilitator. At the time we signed up I thought they were supposed to come with their partners, but by the time it started neither one of them had partners any more.

We probably went to three sessions and given where I was and the stuff I had done in personal development and growth, I felt like I was counseling them.

A big part of this was just my denial, right, not letting anybody help me, but I was there to help everybody else. So I'm telling them all about my finger painting, I mean I had done some pretty introspective pieces of art with my niece Iman.

So I was very "advanced" in terms of coping with it, but not really. I was kind of covering up.

Meredith: Were you also seeing the therapist then, or was that later?

Megan: It was probably at the same time. I saw the therapist 8 times so that had to be over a couple of months. It was in the middle of chemo when I started.

Sharon and I were having some real challenges. My being sick put a huge strain on our relationship. That was the part I really couldn't cope with. I was working with the therapist more on our relationship than my actual experience of having breast cancer.

Both of those women in the lesbian support group were angry.

One was early 40s and the other was our age, so we had that piece in common but they had really different values and beliefs around nutrition and medicine and other things.

I knew a lot when I chose to do what I did and was pretty comfortable with it, and they were really rigid with what they were thinking and I didn't happen to agree with it. That was another point of not feeling connected with them.

It was kind of nice to go but I didn't feel I really got a lot out of it. I felt like I was supporting them and it was kind of tiring, it took a lot to actually be there.

And then I think I was traveling too much really, I was never around to go.

So that was kind of my support group experience.

Meredith: Well you got a lot closer to it than I actually did. Which is kind of interesting because my sister Suzanne established the first support group for young women with breast cancer in Australia years before I was diagnosed.

She was kind of a real pioneer in that whole field and as a psychologist.

So when I got diagnosed and was at the hospital there were a couple of things all linked in to that. She had a young women's group and also at the hospital where I had surgery and at the hospital where I had chemo they had their own sort of general support groups.

They also had this kind of buddy system thing where they try to find someone who is of similar age or background or whatever and match them up to you.

So I was very clear from the beginning when I was diagnosed and discussed it at the hospital that I was not going to a support group.

In my head at the time I thought I didn't need it because I was perfectly capable of coping and being functional about this. I think that was also part of not seeing breast cancer as part of my identity - why would I want to go hang out with a group of women who've all got breast cancer?

I don't want to talk about breast cancer and it's not really part of who I am. This was just a minor inconvenience in the meantime. And so I was very clear that I was not going to any support group.

As well as that whole thing of I don't want to sit in front of a group of people and talk about my issues. Or put myself in a situation where I would be in front of a group of people and start talking about something and get upset in public.

So I was definitely not going to do that. And I was umming, and ahhing over the whole, buddy sort of system thing. They get someone who has had breast cancer to ring you up and try to have a bit of a chat to you.

I thought at least with that you don't have to go anywhere, they ring you so if it doesn't work you can just leave it and let it go.

She eventually rang me and I must have had at least one chemo treatment by then, I was in the middle of my first block of treatment.

I think the basis on which she was selected for me was that she was youngish, she was a bit older than me but had small children so the rationale I suppose was that she could talk about the impact on you and your children and whatever.

So she rang me and I was really not interested in having the conversation. Beyond the fact that we were both young, had children and had breast cancer we had nothing in common.

So her talking about her experience, compared to my experience didn't really work. You know I was working at a reasonably high professional level and struggling with that and just really not being ready to talk about it.

I think I we talked for half an hour or so and we sort of left it that if I needed to speak with her again I would call. I was pretty honest with Suzanne, and said, "Look it just didn't work, she sounded really nice but we really had nothing in common with each other and I'm not ready to talk about it anyway."

Later I met someone else who was diagnosed around the same time as I was, and was at the same hospital for chemo and everything.

She actually went along to a support group - not one of the ones organized by my sister - but one that was run by the hospital. She'd just been diagnosed and really scared, and then when she went to the group it was made up of women who were in all stages of the disease. They had women who were in the terminal stages so can you imagine at that point, you've just been diagnosed, you're just starting your treatment and dealing with all of that, and you get sent to a support group where you are faced with, staring you in the face is your greatest fear.

And there were some quite young women in that group as well. So I think she only went once or twice and just couldn't go anymore.

I discussed that with Suzanne and she said that people in different stages of the disease need different things.

One of the pieces of feedback I gave Suzanne also in reading all of the book lets and support materials was that my first impression was that only straight women get breast cancer.

I was in a pretty bolshy mood at the time, but it really struck me. There was nothing in there that was not specific about having male partners. And just because of who I am and the friends and family I have it was glaring at me.

Thinking about how lesbians feel in that situation with having no resources that related to them.

So I think that in addition to the fact I was not the type to go work things out in groups, I'd rather work it out by myself, it was that none of the support group mechanisms, or the buddy system - they were not people I had anything in common with other than the fact that I had breast cancer.

And I just didn't see that as part of my identity, I didn't want to be associated or around that all the time, but clearly you look at where we are now, we did have stuff we needed to talk about, we just didn't know it at the time. And there was no way or mechanism for that to happen.

When we ended up at the yacht club sitting next to each other and discovered we had both had breast cancer, it obviously triggered more of a connection than other people I'd met.

My memory of how that conversation went is that we were pretty tentative in getting around the whole topic. It took at least another glass of beer to get down to the specifics of what did you have, reconstruction and what ever else.

We got the basic facts of our situations but we really didn't get into any serious discussions for months afterwards. We talked about Tomb Raider, and motorcycles and...

Megan: And the walk, how you'd done it and we were going to do it...

Meredith: Yeah, and how I'd been wanting to do it again so here was a perfect excuse...

And even the next day we didn't discuss breast cancer at all. I remember asking you about triathlons and how long you'd been doing them, and we were talking about sailing and about the walk and other stuff but we didn't go back to a conversation about breast cancer at all.

So that was October/November and then I went to London and to Malaysia and we started emailing pretty much from the time you got back.

And we talked about anything but the fact that we'd had breast cancer. Even when we did it was just clarifying the odd specific here and there.

I think by January we emailed about which drugs we'd had, not what it actually felt like to have chemo.

And it wasn't until you hit the wall in January and you were brave enough to send an email saying you weren't coping but had pretty much been pretending that you were, up to that point.

That got us started on those conversations. But gee, we danced all around it for months. Even in those conversations we had big disclaimers and escape clauses before and after.

Megan: That was pretty funny. We'd spend an entire email talking about how we didn't need a disclaimer, and then the next one would start with one.

Meredith: That's right, so it wasn't until I actually got to the States the first time and started talking that we got past that.

So in terms of the sort of support that works for you what I take out of that is that we had so much else in common that we actually became good friends about all the rest of that.

When the shit hit the fan we were able to go there, but it really was a tentative thing, which was probably part of where we were in the process and not really wanting to go there and deal with it.

I don't know. It's obviously been so important for us to find each other and talk about that.

The medium we used as well of email, that's a great place to hide and run away from stuff. You don't get bailed up on the spot where you can't run from it.

It allows that to sort of happen. This book really documents how that all worked for us. And we've talked about setting up a web-site with our own version of dating software so that people can actually find a friend based on other things - other than the fact you just had cancer.

Someone with the same demographics, with whom you have something in common. And it's a really safe way of sort of testing out and getting to know someone, of providing support. To create something that would give that to more people would have great value.

Megan: I think what creates a big part of that connection is where you are in that breast cancer process.

When I went to Sydney, my specific questions to the world were, "What's next? What does it look like after you've finished treatment?" And I had no idea. It didn't make any sense to me.

One minute you're sick and then the next you're not. How are you actually supposed to make that transition? Because I had to have a plan and know what that looked like.

And so that's exactly what you stepped into. It was like, "Here, I'm already done and I'm doing all this great things."

Meredith: I was doing the whole, "I'm over it and nothing has changed and I've moved on.", routine.

Megan: Right, and that's where you were. You thought, I thought - we both thought we were over it. And there you were, and if I had any lingering questions about how to get over it, there you were just going on and living and doing all these things that were amazing and great.

You were just over it.

And so my meltdown came from two things. It came from setting my goals for the next year that were outside of what I could physically and emotionally deal with given what I'd just been through.

And having my knee go out was really upsetting and depressing because I had to look at not being able to do what I was going to do to prove that I was better than before.

And then finding another lump. Which couldn't have been anything, given when I'd finished chemo.

Meredith: But that's your first reaction.

Megan: Well what I got was a really heavy dose of, "This stuff just doesn't go away.", and it's a part of your identity whether you like it or not. It was the start of that conversation.

Any time I approached it, even though we had danced around all the breast cancer stuff along the way you always responded one for one with whatever I dished out.

So I just started upping the ante as I got stuck. It wasn't like I knew I had this stuff I had to work out and picked you to work it out with.

We had just clicked because of exactly where we were in our recovery and where we were in our lives, and we had a lot of things in common about what was important to us. You know, family and travel and sports. Three huge areas that were things we were never going to let go of.

Meredith: I think part of that too was we because had so much in common it always gave us somewhere to back away to. We could dance around stuff but whenever we needed an out.

It would be a very intense relationship if all we ever spoke about was breast cancer and very limiting.

Megan: And that's not a real experience of life.
              Like if you get buried into one particular
              topic you've limited yourself. That's not
              my definition of living life fully.

Meredith: It wasn't how we saw ourselves anyway,
              of being purely defined by this experience.
              So we have pages and pages of emails on
              inane topics that are only of interest to us
              and had nothing to do with our experience
              of breast cancer.

              There were other places we could go and
              if we needed to we could go back to the
              breast cancer.

Megan: Well you made a great point this morning
              looking at that email where I found that
              lump and was scared and it was a whole
              page, five paragraphs of nonsense before I
              actually spit it out.

              I had it strategically buried inside that
              email. So the other inane topics were
              things you could easily have spent a lot
              of time responding to.

Meredith: Oh it was a very well thought-out and
              crafted email, there was nothing accidental
              about where you dropped it in. I was
              laughing about it at the time.

Megan: No you didn't!

Meredith: Yes I did, I read it through and thought,
              "Whoa...you've been building up to this."

Megan: I gave you every way possible out of it, to
              not have to respond. It would have been

real easy for you to say, "Oh well, don't worry about it, I've been there too."

But instead you actually opened up and looked at your experience in a way you hadn't looked at it before. And you shared with me what it's really like.

Meredith: After I'd been telling you for six months it's easy, you just get over it.

But that was part of it for me. I'd been playing that role in my head for so long that this forced me to get real.

That's what you were for me in reverse, someone who had the same approach, was going out and doing triathlons and traveling.

Really where we are now is because you were brave enough to admit that you weren't coping.

Megan: Well it was just one of those things where stuff would come spilling out without really knowing where it was going and you would come right back with your honesty that would let it go beyond superficial comments. It took two to end up where we are now.

Travel

*I don't want to get to the end of my life and
find that I have just lived the length of it.
I want to have lived the breadth of it as well.*

DIANE ACKERMAN

Megan's Trip to Montana:
Live Conversation - Las Vegas, October 2003

Meredith: So why did you decide to go to Montana
straight after surgery, was that something
pre-arranged or spur of the moment?

Megan: I think the trip had actually been booked
the month before that. Sharon and I were
supposed to go for the Fourth of July to
see family who had a cabin in Montana,
near Yellowstone.

It was 10 days after surgery when we
went. When I was diagnosed it still seemed
like a great idea - you know my romantic
vision of healing - we'll go off into the
woods, and stay in a cabin, and get in
touch with nature. It would be a place for
me to read and write, and hike and recover.

At the time I was feeling pretty good
actually. I was recovering from the surgery
faster than I thought. I'd been for a run,

I think a week after surgery, a couple of days before the trip.

I was still upset about having missed the triathlon and I was trying to stay in shape. It had taken me months to get to what I thought was a decent level of fitness and I didn't want to go backwards because its so hard to get it back. Two years later now I've still not got that back.

The only problem I had at the time was that my chest was collecting fluid. That was uncomfortable and it kind of sloshed around when I ran. I called my surgeon before I left to say this is what's happening, is it OK if I travel?

She said some fluid retention was normal and it would eventually be assimilated, and it should be perfectly fine for me to travel. Of course, I tend to understate things. I think I probably had more fluid than I conveyed in that conversation because I really wanted to go on the trip.

So she said no problem, and I got the OK to make the trip, and we went.

It was one of those hard to get to places. We flew into Billings, and then we had a three hour drive. We went over this 11,000 ft mountain pass - I remember getting to the top of the mountain and there was still snow even though it was July.

So I had to get out and play in the snow - in my flip flops and shorts - because what else would you do?

We got there and we had a choice of where to stay. They had a house with a few bedrooms and a couple of bathrooms and full kitchen, but we stayed at the place they called "The Ritz".

It was this little short hike through the woods away from the main house to a little one room cabin. To get into the bed you had to climb up a ladder, there was a wood stove, and an outhouse.

The outhouse was far enough away that you couldn't go at night because there were bears. They showed us all the bear marks on all the trees around the cabin, so we had a chamber pot instead. It was quite an adventure!

Meredith: So what did you do there?

Megan: Well we went for hikes. I can remember doing push ups, which is sort of a classic little story. We took our weight bands and did our exercises. The best part is that I could do more straight leg pushups than Sharon, still only two weeks out from having a mastectomy!

I don't know if that was the smartest thing to do, but it felt pretty good. And I had all the breast cancer books with me, but I couldn't actually bring myself to read them.

I do remember reading an article on lymphedema and thinking, "I really don't want this." You know, don't do this, don't do that...all the things I was doing like the pushups. I don't want this but I'm not going to stop doing what I want to anyway.

My chest got progressively more annoying, because we would go for hikes, and I wasn't wearing a bra at all, so it was "slosh, slosh, slosh". Uncomfortable.

There was a creek out the back, and they would talk about having all these parties where people would go and strip down and jump in the water. It was fresh mountain water - I think we were staying at 7,000 feet.

So I thought that would be a cool thing, that we would go jump in the creek. We put on our bathing suits and we went and sat in the creek. It was freezing cold so I just sat down and splashed water over my head and then got out and went to take a shower.

Meredith: I gather from our other conversations that this didn't turn out to be a healing dip in a mountain stream?

Megan: It was supposed to be. The next day we went for a drive and we went into Yellowstone and stopped at the gift shop. I started feeling really feverish and light-headed.

I had no sense of balance. So I went outside where it was cooler and sat on the steps and just felt really dizzy and hot. I remember my chest being really hot to the touch but I really didn't think too much about it or make any connection.

So we kept going and finally got to this resort we'd been heading to - hot springs, of all things! We went in the bar and I just couldn't sit up, I couldn't get comfortable, there was nowhere to lay down, there were too many people.

I just felt horrible. In the end, we went into the lobby and there was a sofa there and I slept for several hours. We eventually left and drove the three hours back to the cabin.

The next day I couldn't get out of bed. I was in excruciating pain, just really sick. I slept all day. Sharon finally took my temperature that evening. It was 103.5 F. I was burning up.

Eventually we got a neighbor who volunteered to drive us down over the mountain. There was no way I could do it obviously and Sharon couldn't do it at night. It was a scary road.

We really needed to go to the hospital. I didn't want to see a local doctor because I didn't trust that they would understand my surgery or be able to diagnose whatever was going on with me.

The neighbor drove us over the hill really fast because he was a local and he had grown up there. Sharon got car sick so he named one of the hairpin turns after her, when we finally got to the bottom and she got out to puke her guts out!

We got to the emergency room in Billings at two in the morning and saw a nurse, and then one of the local doctors. He said that they happened to have a surgeon and if I wanted to wait until he got out of whatever surgery he was doing, he could see me.

I felt really happy when he came in because he was familiar with mastectomies, he just seemed like a really competent doctor. I felt much better because I had all this fluid and I really didn't want someone learning on me how to aspirate it.

He sucked out about 9 ounces of fluid and sent it off to the lab. I had an open wound basically and had jumped in that creek, so I ended up with a nice infection.

I got some antibiotics and we went and stayed in a motel and flew out the next day. Sharon had to push me around the airport in a wheelchair. Mom took me to see my surgeon when I got home. I remember being in the doctor's office and I couldn't sit up on the table.

It was really upsetting because I'd been so determined that the surgery wouldn't slow me down, it just wasn't going to be a big deal. Then I was so sick I couldn't do anything.

The first surgeon had ordered some lab work done on the fluid taken out. It turned out to be a a very scary staph infection and my surgeon decided that the antibiotics he had given me weren't going to be enough so she prescribed a double dose of Cipro.

Which is the anthrax drug, and that was all in the news at the time, so I thought I could save some and sell them on the black market! Everyone wanted a stash of Cipro in their closet.

So a few days later with Mom and Shannon I flew to Illinois for our annual family trip.

Meredith: It didn't put you off traveling?

Megan: Nope! And I was sick, I was on heavy duty antibiotics, and I had to take naps - you know how much I hate naps.

So when I was seeing my surgeon she was horrified to learn what I'd been doing. Horrified to hear I'd been in the creek, and horrified to hear I'd been doing push ups.

I said to her, "You said I could do anything I wanted!" She said, "Well for most women that means brushing their hair." I thought, "OK, we obviously have a communication problem here!"

So Mom went down a list, "Can she do this, can she do that?" It turned out I could ride a stationary bike if I wanted to and that was about it. I could not lift my niece, who was a year and a half. I could have left that question out, personally.

Then Mom followed me around Illinois. "You can't lift her up. You can't lift that luggage!"

It was really frustrating because I couldn't actually do anything.

I remember we were in some city in Kentucky and I had to read a map. I was usually the navigator and I had to get us across this little town, and I just couldn't read the map.

I had a huge meltdown, I was just sobbing. I just had this fear of what if it never came back - my whole identity was tied up in being smart and quick. What if I couldn't do the things that I relied on?

It was just devastating, and I think that was the first time I saw breast cancer as limiting me.

I couldn't face that and I'm not sure that I've faced it yet. I really don't want to believe that my brain doesn't work as well as it did before.

Meredith: You know all through my treatment I ran around and did insane things - traveled to the U.S., Papua New Guinea and India, and sailed - really at the time you shouldn't be able to do those things physically, but somehow you find the will power to manage it.

And it wasn't until after my treatment when John and I went on our trip to Italy and Greece that I got a reality check about my physical limitations.

On Santorini we went on a sunset cruise around the caldera, and they take you to the little volcano in the middle, which was really cool.

And it's only a 15 minute walk up to the top to actually look down where all the lava and stuff is going on and we just got there on the boat and I said to John, "I just can't do it. I'm not going to be able to get up the hill, and you just go on." He was a sweetheart and stayed with me on the boat.

And that was the first time that I had actually caved in and admitted that I couldn't do it.

We went to Sorrento in Italy and did a day cruise in a little fishing boat, and sailed into this little bay where there was a grotto you could swim into with a fluorescent ceiling, and I had to say again that I couldn't do it because I didn't think I could swim in there and out again.

So that was kind of hard, and I've got the same issues as you with how my memory is and not feeling as sharp as I was before. I certainly don't have as good a recall and my map reading has gone to hell.

Meredith's Trip to India: Email Conversation

From: Megan
Sent: Saturday, February 01, 2003

I wanted to thank you for sharing the photos from India. What an amazing project. I can see why you kept working through treatment. I'll bet you had an amazing bond with those incredible kids. You weren't worried about being so far from home and doctors? Brave woman. After my infection in Montana, I made sure I knew where the nearest hospital was on all of my future jaunts.

From: Meredith
Sent: Saturday, February 01, 2003

India was an interesting experience health wise! I was supposed to go the November of the year I got sick, but obviously had to cancel. It had taken 8 months that year to work in all of the required immunizations, so when I finally finished chemo the big question was whether any of that immunity would have survived. In the end it was too late to start the injections again and expect that they would do any good, so we just winged it. My boss had had two heart bypass operations, so his health was dodgy too, so we had the best medical insurance and evacuation cover money could buy.

I was careful what I ate (took lots of museli bars with me to get through the day!) and only drank bottled water from the hotel. The funniest experience was after our first visit to an orphanage for girls - I literally had kids crawling all over me all day, and then when we got in the truck to go home the Director pulled us aside and told us to have a really hot shower when we got back to the hotel because most of the kids had skin diseases.

I felt like saying, "HELLOOOO...IMUNO SUPPRESSED PERSON HERE!" Visiting the slums was interesting too because there is no sewage in India anywhere outside of the hotels - you drive along the roads and people are just squatting by the side of the street.

One slum we went to we had to walk from the highway down this long dusty dirt alley and all along the side there were people relieving themselves beside us.

The only time I got sick was in Singapore on the way home when I was craving for a burger - it had a nasty reaction I think because after two weeks of rice it was a bit much.

Meredith's Trip to India:
Live Conversation - Las Vegas, October 2003

Meredith: Travel has always been a big part of my life and what I loved to do, particularly in the last couple of years travelling internationally.

At the time I was diagnosed it was about three weeks I think before I was supposed to travel to India for the first time, which was something I had been really looking forward to and preparing for a long time.

I'd already had the eight months of immunisations to get there. And I knew that the programs that we were funding over there were amazing and I really wanted to see them, and it was an exotic foreign country.

In November I was supposed to go to London to present at a conference, which was the leading international conference in my particular area of expertise, so that was quite a big deal for me as well.

Then I got diagnosed, and I think one of the immediate bummers out of all of that was that I was not going to be able to make those trips. Probably not the primary concern, but it was a significant source of annoyance for me.

The way my treatment panned out was I knew I was out of circulation for potentially 10 months, which was really frustrating because I didn't know if there was going to be another opportunity to go back to India.

The people I was to travel with went in any case, so I'd clearly missed that trip.

I think the first opportunities came up when I'd finished my first three months of chemo and I was in the middle of radiation treatment, or coming towards the end of that.

Two things came up. One was that I had been working on a foundation that was being established to work with poor kids overseas, and Papua New Guinea was a key area that we had been doing work in.

It's a hugely disadvantaged country with very high poverty rates, and we had programs there that were working with kids who otherwise would not have an opportunity for an education or better life.

It's also a place that has some family associations for me because my grandfather had fought in World War II in Papua New Guinea and he'd never talked about what it was like for him up there.

He wasn't on the Kokoda Trail, which is the famous battle ground there that saved Australia from Japanese invasion in WWII, he was in Port Moresby as an air force mechanic.

So I had some sort of curiosity about that.

At the same time, it's not the safest place in the world to visit. They have serious law and order problems up there. There are groups of bandits called the "Rascals", who run around, generally pillage and create mayhem, and in particular attack foreigners who are visiting.

So I had the opportunity to go there, and that was in the middle of radiation because the way my treatment worked out was that I went five days a week.

Except one day a fortnight I got off, because they have to service the machines. So I had 5 days on, and the next week I had 4 days on.

I could actually manoeuvre around to get a three day clear patch which is what I did for Port Moresby.

So I went up there. I didn't tell my mother I was going. John was very indulgent in letting me go there, particularly considering there had been riots two weeks before I went, in the very suburb that I was to visit.

It's actually an area where the U.S. Peace Corps had pulled its volunteers out of two years beforehand because it was too dangerous.

Megan: Did you ever think about not going?

Meredith: No. I think, apart from the fact that I love to travel, I think that there was this real pig-headedness and resentment that my illness had stopped me from travelling.

It was something that I really wanted to do, and I was going to go. I don't think I really had a sense of how dangerous it was until I got there.

Which certainly caused me pause, and it won't be high on my list of holiday spots for some years. The Australian government has just made a commitment to sending a police force up there to try to sort it out, so hopefully that will help.

I had a reasonable amount of hair back that had grown during radiation after my first lot of chemo. We were picked up at the airport by a car which we'd arranged to take us to the hotel.

It was quite nice. It was opposite the foreigners and ex-pat's enclave, which had eight foot high security fences and razor wire around it.

Drove through the Central Business District with bars on all the windows, and knocked out windows, and there was a curfew in place.

We got into the hotel and I was thinking things weren't too bad. The next morning our host came to pick us up in his truck with cracked front and rear windscreens.

Of course I leapt into the front seat with him. We headed down the road and I said, "What happened to the car?"

He said, "Oh, I came home last night and the rascals were standing in the driveway with a shotgun, but I floored the engine and took off past them so they didn't manage to shoot me, they threw bricks."

It turned out to not be an uncommon experience for them to be held up at shotgun point. One of my other bosses was held up on the side of the road there with a shotgun a few months back.

So that also gave me some pause, and my cell phone didn't work there, which really made me uneasy. Although, mind you, the fact is that even if you could call someone there, the ambulance service stopped working months ago because they ran out of money to pay their petrol bills.

So the chances of anyone coming to rescue me would be pretty slim.

Our programs there hadn't had a phone service for 6 months because it just broke down and there was no one to fix it. So there is a complete break down of services.

It was a really interesting trip. There wasn't a lot of opportunity, though, to really interact with the kids. They were very shy and reserved.

There had been a really violent incident at the school that morning where a guy had beaten a woman so badly she ended up in hospital, before he ran off into the bush. Which the kids had actually witnessed.

They were undoubtedly a bit traumatised so it was pretty hard to make a connection with them.

That was a three day trip, and I was kind of pleased to leave. It's a great program there, but not a particularly easy place to visit.

Around that time, I was also given the opportunity to go to a workshop and series of meetings in San Francisco, for which I moved heaven and earth and treatment to make sure I could go.

Being able to work in some capacity was always important to me all the way through being sick, so making that trip work was a big deal.

Then there was India.

It was probably around that time that I was having radiation that my boss started talking about another trip back to India, and I really wanted to go. I think he probably manipulated the dates to try and work around when I would have actually finished treatment.

I flew there about 5 weeks after I had finished chemo.

My oncologist was pretty well unconcerned. I went to see my GP because I had missed my last lot of shots for India when I got diagnosed.

We had some discussion about what degree of my immunity would have remained from my previous inoculations. I could have had a blood test done to see, but it was really going to be too late to do anything.

I couldn't have any immunizations while I was having chemo because they're all live viruses. And my immune system was still so suppressed in the lead up to going that it wasn't really worth trying.

We decided not to do the blood tests and just not know, and assume that I still had some immunity, and wing it and hope for the best.

I think part of the drive in insisting on going to India was to get back what I'd lost. The fact that I'd had to cancel that trip because I was sick, so that was a big motivator.

John was really supportive in not wondering what the hell his wife was doing running off to this third world country when she was so sick. I think he knew it was really important to me to do.

And once again, it was part of doing my job, this was what I'd been working towards when I got sick, and I wanted to finish it.

Megan: Was there any significance in it being at the end of your treatment?

Meredith: I think the significance was really about getting back something I'd lost. India was at the beginning of August, and in September/October John and I went to Italy and Greece.

And that trip was always my target through treatment, in that I'm going to get through this awful experience and then go with John to Greece and Italy for a month and have a fabulous time.

I was certainly very conscious, it was one of the things when I was actually in the hospital having chemo treatments of counting them down and thinking each one got me that much closer to that trip.

That was my reward.

When I got there India had an impact on me that I didn't really expect. I don't think you can prepare yourself for a place like that.

It's a culture that is so different and a level of poverty, and a society that operates in a way that is so different from your experience.

Even in Mumbai (Bombay) which is a huge city. I think it was even a culture shock from other parts of Asia I'd visited. I'd spent a lot of time in Thailand and Bangkok, other places, but in Mumbai the poverty was abject and in your face as soon as you got off the plane.

I was very conscious of what I was going to be able to eat and drink over there. I had a suitcase packed full of muesli bars, not my favourite food of choice, but I thought at least I'd have something I could eat.

Always having bottled water, because my immune system was still really shaky. The first night in Mumbai we checked into a hotel and there was no bottled water, so I brushed my teeth with Coke.

Completely self defeating, but at least I felt like I'd made an effort!

We got down to Madurai in the south, where 70% of the population lives in poverty. We went out and visited these projects working with women and children who are in the lowest caste, the Untouchables, in India.

They have incredible challenges in their lives, living in an area where your only real worth in the family is economic.

Female children don't have a great deal of worth because they are an expensive liability down the line, in terms of dowry. So there is a high rate of female infanticide.

We went to a school on our first day - no chairs, no desks, no books. Bare cement floors and walls.

They had their students - all about 10 years old - acting out little scenes of social problems in the area. So we came to these two little girls, and one was sitting on the floor holding a baby doll, and the other was standing trying to pull the doll out of her arms.

And the Principal explained to us that they were acting out female infanticide. It just stopped me absolutely cold. Imagining what it must be like to be a little girl growing up in a village, and a baby is born next door, and it's a girl, and that child is murdered and there is no justice or retribution.

What does that do to your sense of self-worth, or security or importance?

We run shelters there for young girls who have been abandoned by their families because they are inconvenient. Street kids who had run away from home after watching their fathers beat their mothers to death. Rescuing child labourers from factories. Supporting disabled kids.

I saw how those kids and women live with dignity and hope in the midst of incredible poverty and hardship. Being positive about their future and taking every opportunity they could was a huge thing for me at that time.

Having thought that I'd gone through hell for 10 months, it was nothing compared to what these people lived with every day of their lives.

And they live with a great deal of uncertainty too, in terms of their health and their income and their personal safety. So it was an incredibly moving experience for me to go and see people living in those circumstances and how they moved on beyond that.

It had a big impact on me in thinking about how I would move forward from what I'd been through.

Certainly there was some sense of completion in having actually, finally made that trip and doing what I had been prevented from doing before.

Much the same as 12 months later when I got to go back to London and present at that conference that I'd had to skip the first time around.

That was a big thing for me - almost ticking off a list of things I needed to do.

The trip that John and I did in September/October 2001 to Italy and Greece, that was really about celebrating life and putting it all behind us.

Life was now back on track because that is what we did in our life - we traveled. We had gone to Italy four months before I was diagnosed, a place that we loved and it was one of the good things in our life.

So that was kind of the intention. It became a weird trip because we were in Greece on September 11 when everything was falling apart, and that added a layer of stress and surrealism to the trip.

It was probably on that trip that I got a real sense of how run down I was and my physical limitations.

I must have been running on pure adrenaline in India, because I shouldn't have been able to do what I did there. You shouldn't be able to spend 12 hours a day on the road in 40 degree (104 F) heat not eating anything other than muesli bars and drinking water when you're in that physical state.

You shouldn't be able to do that, but I did.

Megan: Sounds like my triathlon!

Meredith: Yep. Maybe I was starting to come back down to reality by the time I got to Greece and Italy.

Megan: What do you think changes that? Was it that in Italy and Greece you were just wanting to enjoy yourself, but in India it was still part of the survival mentality, and your determination - a sense of having to make up for something?

Meredith: I think it was just a big reality check. I had this idea through treatment that once I finished I was going to be the same person I was before.

When I went to India, I still looked like absolute crap, I had no hair virtually and was kind of struggling, but I expected to. I was only just out of chemo.

I think what started to happen was that I was getting full on back into work at the time, going into the office every day, and what I discovered was that I could make it till about 2:00 p.m. in the afternoon and I was exhausted.

So I think by September I was getting a real reality check about how long it was going to take to get back to what I thought was normal.

Megan: I'm thinking about January when I had a huge emotional breakdown and it was three months after I had finished chemo, about the same time frame.

The reference that I don't have, is that because I hadn't been working a normal job before, and I didn't go back to a normal job, I didn't have that comparison.

As someone who is self-employed, and in theory self-motivated, it's never really been an issue for me. I didn't really have a sense of how hard I work, or how much am I able to do.

I know that I wasn't able to do as much as I wanted to, but I didn't have a direct comparison, I'm definitely more tired than I was before.

Meredith: With a 9 to 5 job it was immediately apparent to me, that I couldn't do it...

Megan: I just felt like a wimp, like, why am I not
            doing these things that obviously need
            to be done, and no real structure to iden-
            tify what was going on.

            I don't really remember having naps, but
            I didn't have a structure for my day, so if
            I slept in, I slept in. If I went to bed early,
            I went to bed early.

Meredith: You know I was going to bed at 7:30 p.m.
            at night for what seemed like a year. 8:30
            p.m. if I stretched it. That killed me.

            Even now I won't have that many late
            nights in a week.

            It was such a dramatic change from life
            beforehand. It was really frustrating - I
            had the same bedtime as my 8 year old son!

How Do I Get Through This?

*You gain strength, courage and confidence by
every experience in which
you really stop to look fear in the face.
You are able to say to yourself,
"I have lived through the horror. I can take the next
thing that comes along."
You must do the thing you think you cannot do.*

ELEANOR ROOSEVELT

Coping:
Live Conversation - California, October 2003

Meredith: There's a whole physical side to getting
through the chemo process and there's
also a whole mental side to getting your
self through that treatment.

What you think when you are told you
are going to have to go through this for
the next three months. At the time I was
diagnosed and was told what my treatment would be I was not looking forward
to it with any degree of trepidation.

You can see it in my email that I sent
out to people - I just saw it as this great
challenge. "Oh cool, you get 10 months
now to really test yourself!"

At that stage the whole cancer experience
to me was just about the treatment. There
was never any thought that there was any
emotional or mental process to cope with
further down the track.

I remember talking to people and sending them emails at the time saying that I was actually looking forward to it, you know, getting in there and fighting the cancer, and kicking its butt and doing it in a really strong way. Do it better than anybody else, in a competitive kind of way.

I think when I went in the first time I was in this really hyper, pumped up competitive frame of mind. Go ahead, give it your best shot and I will be better than this, and stronger than this, whatever you reckon the side effects are.

I was on this real adrenaline high. I was certainly aware in the car on the way home of feeling a bit out of sorts with all the drugs and everything else but when I got home I said, "I actually feel quite good."

I was feeling on top of it and coping, and John was with me and we had a really good day at home together, and the day after.

And I was thinking, well this is a piece of cake really, not such a big deal at all.

But as it went on, I really didn't like people sticking needles in my veins, and it was harder going in the second time. And certainly after that I was absolutely aware of the huge mental push it took to make myself go in there.

Because I really didn't feel well after I'd had chemo and I knew I was getting worse and more run down.

So the mental battle, knowing that it was coming up...you just start to feel better and you have to go back in again and be made to feel worse.

By the last shot, it really is an intense mental struggle to make yourself get up and go in there, knowing from past experience you are going to get stuffed around and you are going to get needles stuck into your veins half a dozen times because they can't find the right one.

It hurts like hell - the needles, and the drug going in - you can feel it burning. The worst was the Taxol, that really hurt. You know they have those instructions about letting them know if you're feeling any unnecessary pain?

OK, well it hurts sticking the needle in and the drug burns. When is there something unusual that I should actually be reporting here?

At the end of the first round of chemo that was the night I got really sick, which was a combination I think of the physical as well as the mental overload.

The second round of chemo, the Taxol, was even worse to go through the second time around.

So how do you keep yourself distracted through this whole process and not thinking about what's going on?

I had the whole thing about going to the gym while I was having chemo. Which started out about getting my shoulder moving and also about the lymphedema thing and wanting to make sure that didn't happen and I could go sailing.

But it actually became a key part of keeping me moving so I wasn't sitting around for three weeks waiting for the next shot of chemo and thinking about that.

There was certainly work I was doing in the meantime, and I was working to the capacity that I had. But I was going to the gym within a day or two of having chemo, and going two to three times a week.

And it was really tough to get through a work out, but when ever I did I had this enormous feeling of satisfaction that I had done it, that I was doing something and achieving somehow.

There were days though when I just couldn't get up and out and do anything. So what do you do then to distract yourself?

I had cable TV, and really good absorbing shows like Law & Order - back to back episodes at midday. I never stayed on to watch NYPD afterwards because they had that story arc where one of the main characters was dying at the time.

I had my PlayStation which I played to death. I went through all three Tomb Raider games that were available at the time. It's a role playing game where you are powerful, and kicking butt, doing stuff. It's engaging your brain and you can't think about anything else while you are doing it, other than playing that game.

So in terms of strategies for me to get through treatment, it was important for me to get out of the house, otherwise I would have been completely consumed with why I was stuck in the house. Getting out to the gym gave me a reason for that.

And when I couldn't manage that there was something else to completely absorb me so I was not thinking about what I was dealing with.

Work was important too. For the first 4 or 5 hours after a chemo shot the anti-nausea drugs and steroids were so good I usually didn't feel too bad. So I would go and have chemo and then come home and actually send emails and do work stuff, it was completely insane.

I would do it before I went, and I'd do it when I got home so at least I had some sense that work hadn't stopped.

Megan: I was thinking about my first chemo treatment and that was when I figured out there was more mental stuff.

Well, I know your mental outlook is a big factor in anything, so one of the things that was available to me was through one of the support groups we went to.

There was this woman who did basically a form of hypnosis as a way of coping. And so I went and had a private session with her and she made, like a personal tape.

What were my concerns around chemo - and she made this personal hypnosis tape where you basically go and do a deep breath relaxation and it talks about how the chemo only attacks the cells that it needed to attack and the rest of you is perfectly well. The tape makes me sick now.

But it fit in right with my beliefs at the time and so it was a way of protecting myself from my fear of "this is going to do more harm than good", which really was my biggest fear. I was worried about intentionally doing something that I think is going to do more harm than good.

There's an off-chance it's going to do some good. And so it was just a layer of protective armour, you know, I could just plug this in for the first hour and maybe it would set me up for something positive.

And it certainly got me relaxed enough to sit there through the stuff.

So after the first treatment I went home and then they called me and said they'd screwed up and not given me enough and I had to go back.

That was when it struck me that this was going to be really emotionally challenging as I completely fell apart. And I'd gotten home feeling pretty good and I wasn't trying to work, but I was just laying there and sort of, you know, being OK being sick. I didn't feel that bad, but I think it was just the emotional drain. I just wanted to watch TV and kind of see what would happen. And then when they called I just fell completely apart, and had to go back the next day.

That was really hard. And then as each subsequent treatment went on, I would get really wigged out about four days beforehand.

Because what happened was I'd feel awful for the first week, and then even the first four days are the worst, and then I'd start feeling better and start doing stuff.

And then by the end of the three weeks I could do anything, or so I thought. That would be the time when I would start running again, and that would be the time I could go water skiing and that was the time when I felt pretty strong and OK.

The thought of going back and having to revert back to this invalid kind of a role became really depressing, and so I would just be nasty, cranky...really upset. It was miserable the four days leading into the next treatment.

I was working at the time but only with the clients I had, I wasn't out drumming up new business, because I didn't know if I would be able to take care of them, which was a constant fear of mine.

Just not having the strength or the confidence, I don't know. I didn't want to go out and talk to new people, I just didn't have it in me.
What I did manage to do was watch my niece Iman for three days a week. She was about a year and a half at the time.

So I'd drive over to Shannon's house three days a week and play with Iman. I didn't really have a choice other than to be up.

There were some days when I really couldn't get up and about so I just convinced her to watch TV with me.

I only had her for an hour in the morning and then I'd drive her to school, then go pick her up and drive her back. So it wasn't until the very last chemo when I was so sick. I made it over there but then I couldn't physically watch her. Thank God she was sleeping so both of us slept all morning.

Like you were saying, the need to get out of the house and what is it that you are going to be able to get out of the house to do.

So for me, setting up meetings and to go and meet with clients and to have to function intelligently in an area that was new to me, and I was really sort of self conscious about not knowing everything, that didn't work for me.

It had to be something that was compel ling enough and comfortable enough that I wanted to go and do it. Like to go and play with Iman. There's something about a baby that is irresistible, so I did more things physically than I would have otherwise.

My default was Law & Order, and back-to-backs were great. I didn't have the benefit of a PlayStation, but certainly TV was the thing to numb the brain.

Meredith: Why do you think Law & Order worked so well for us?

Megan: Well, I actually read in Oprah magazine, in times of crisis or trauma or high stress, the brain wants something that's really formulaic, and repetitive, and easy to grasp, and familiar, and Law & Order was a specific example they gave of a TV show that works really well in trauma.

Meredith: Really? You know I was just thinking that we are both strong, independent women, and you are going through this awful thing that feels like its sapping your strength but you have to power your way through.

So 95% of the time in that show, the good guys win, they have really strong female characters - OK, lets be honest, our favourite Law & Order is with Angie Harmon who was the best kick-ass ADA in the whole program.

Megan: Absolutely!

Meredith: So you got to watch this program that switched off all the processing in your head, you are absorbed in this classic genre of the good guys versus the bad guys, a bit of mystery, and a strong female protagonist.
Who 95% of the time won, and if she didn't, it was Jack's fault!

Megan: Always!

Meredith: So it's a good powerful role model at a time that you're really not feeling that great or strong about yourself as well.

Megan:	And that's the same thing that made Tomb Raider so powerful for me, I can't tell you how many times I watched that movie when I was sick.
	And Charlie's Angels - it's light, you don't have to think too hard about it, the good guys win, it's very empowering.
	Your mind is great because even when you are laying there unable to move, you can watch people kick butt and step into that role in your head.
Meredith:	That was the great thing about playing Lara Croft on the PlayStation, you could kick the crap out of someone who desperately deserved it.
	So in all of those shows you've got strong, empowered women, and beyond the storyline you've got actors like Angelina Jolie who is a woman who is very strong in her own mind about who she is and doesn't care what anybody else thinks about her.
	She just lives her life and does what is important to her. She's had struggles and difficult times in her life and just gets back up again and gets on with it.
	It was all good stuff to focus on at the time, strong role models and a bit of escapism.
Megan:	Any metaphor you hear about fighting cancer is very sort of warlike and militant and I didn't really embrace that well, but at the same time this idea of fighting something and being really strong was there.

Meredith: I'm just thinking that one of my other favourite TV shows before I got sick was Survivor and I would have loved to have been on it - that whole concept of testing yourself.

I think by the time I was having chemo the second series was on and in Australia they did a local version of the show, and so we were watching the American version and these ads came up on TV for "send in your audition tape" for the Australian show.

And immediately John turned around and said, "Don't you even think about it!"

What really strikes me now in looking at that is that they make a big deal about how tough it is for people to go through that, and I just think well, you have no idea.

How hellish to be stranded on a Tahitian island for 40 days with only rice to eat, you lose a lot of weight and there are whatever psychological challenges to deal with.

That is nothing like going through three months of chemo, let alone doing that twice, the whole physical debilitation that takes place and the mental struggle all the way through to keep going, and keep going back.

Let's see that as reality TV, and they would never actually show it because that's real hard, that's the real edge.

Megan: What's in the background is the whole mortality thing. It's a shock up front and then you are getting treated for some thing that could kill you.

Meredith: And there's no way of getting off THAT island and getting voted out of it. You're stuck there, there is no out.

Megan: And you're pretty much on your own.

Meredith: Also it's not your choice. You know you make the choice to go do triathlons, or regattas or to get yourself marooned on Survivor, but you've got no choice in this.

It just happens to you and you've got to do the best you can to deal with this and there is no way you can opt out, and say, "I think I've had enough now, and I've grown through this experience and I'd like to leave now!"

Megan: I tried that but there's no choice!

Meredith: It's exactly what you said in your triathlon story, that there is no choice but to go on.

You've got to find whatever way works for you. You've got to keep some momentum I think, that was the thing that kept me driving back to the gym.

So even though your health is deteriorating, I felt that by going to the gym at least I was doing something and I would be in better shape than if I wasn't.

I think continuing to go to the gym and feeling like I was working towards a goal, it gave me some sense of momentum instead of just feeling like I was getting sicker all the time.

I knew when I got through this I was going to India, and John and I had our end of chemo trip to Europe planned. Not just something to look forward to, but that you were actively doing something about it.

Megan: Well Australia was definitely a goal that kept me going that gave me something to look forward to after treatment, and at the same time I knew I was going to be physically challenged because of what I wanted to do.

I think we'd been training to sail for two years, and we still had regular sailing meets, so I scheduled my chemo around it.

So if we had a practice weekend coming up I would move a Friday chemo to Monday. I couldn't sail right after chemo and it was really important for me to go and be with the team, and to get out on the water.

And that was with the end in mind, that we are going to this regatta and I need to prepare, even if it's only just being in that environment in the boat.

And I wouldn't have run as much as I did but I definitely felt a real strong pull to do that, based on a deadline. Knowing that I had something coming up after chemo that I was going to have to be somewhat physical for.

It helped me do more than I would have otherwise.

I was thinking the very first email I sent after diagnosis was to my business coach, and I said, "Well, how the hell am I supposed to build this stupid business now I have cancer?"

She sent back a really practical email, which I appreciated, and basically her philosophy was, "Keep an oar in the water."

It doesn't matter how much effort you are putting in to this, but you keep doing something so the momentum keeps going forward. So there is some progress, no matter how little.

It's not like you've abandoned it completely. To have to go back and restart that momentum is really difficult. I did that in all areas of my life, I kept those things going that were important to me so that when I had the energy to go back to them, there was something to build on.

Part III:

What Happens Next?

Meredith's Avon Walk, Florida 2002

*Courage is the price that life exacts
for granting us peace.*

AMELIA EARHART

Meredith's Journal

Day Zero - April 18, 2002

Made it into Miami late yesterday afternoon and made an emergency dash to a sports store to replace all the walking gear lost by our L.A. hotel.

We were late catching the train to Boca Raton after a wrangle over getting our luggage stored for the next three days. Dropped off our gear at the new hotel in Boca and then headed off to register for tomorrow's walk.

What an experience! The walk and registration are a huge logistical exercise - really blown away by the professionalism of the event and the staff.

Already it's clear there is a special vibe among the participants. Part of registration was sitting through an orientation and safety video in a huge auditorium.

While we were waiting for it to begin, several women who had reached their donation target were walking down the aisles offering their extra donations to women who hadn't raised enough.

One of them gave us a $500 cheque to boost our total. An absolutely amazing sense of community.

Just as the video started, some women behind us who had done the walk before said, "Here we go, get ready to cry!"

They were absolutely right! We saw an incredibly moving video from Avon about the walk and the cause, and the personal commitment of everyone from the President of the company down.

During the video we were told that 245 women would die in the US from breast cancer in the three days we would be walking. Really brought the message home.

I cried through it all - starting to think this event is going to be one hell of an emotional roller coaster.

Got back to the hotel late and am attempting to get as much sleep as I can before a 4:30 a.m. start tomorrow.

Day One - April 19, 2002

Wow. What a day. Up at 5:00 a.m. and on a bus to the start of the walk. Met an group of incredible Floridian women on the bus. Mara, Susan, Janet, Pam, Debbie, and would you believe it - Barbie and Cindy (yes, both blonde). Between them they had raised over $15,000 U.S. to take part in the event.

They were blown away to hear that we had come all the way from Australia to walk. I told them that I was a fundraiser who had come to research the event - really didn't feel comfortable saying that I was a survivor.

Somehow I still don't feel that is part of who I am, or who I say I am.

When we all got to the stage for the Opening Ceremony the girls told me that Janet (my age with two small kids) was a breast cancer survivor - I was so stunned I immediately blurted out that I was too.

The first time I think that I've met someone else who not only was a survivor, but who I felt I could relate to at some level.

The Opening Ceremony was incredibly moving - led by a breast cancer survivor who had lost her mother, a sister, aunts and a grandmother to breast cancer, but was a 5 year survivor. She read an opening poem followed by a procession through the middle of the crowd by a small group of women forming a circle. The empty space in the middle of the circle represented all the people participants had lost to breast cancer.

By that stage I was crying again along with everyone around me.

We then took off on Day One - a 19.6 mile (31.5 km) walk - an amazing sight in the early morning light - this huge mass of people linked by a common purpose, experience and emotion.

The range of women there was amazing - so many were wearing shirts with pictures of mothers, daughters, sisters who had died of breast cancer. There were three women who were doing all 13 3-Day walks in the States in memory of their mother.

Every 1-2 miles there was a pit stop with water, Gatorade, snacks and Porta-loos. It was about a 30C

(86F) day and we had been warned to drink at least one bottle of water between each stop - if we weren't using the Porta-loos we weren't drinking enough. "Drink, drink, pee, pee and no IV" signs were everywhere - when we got to the first lunch stop we found out why.

At lunch the triage tent had 8 IVs hooked up to people who had become dehydrated. We found out at camp tonight that 6 people had been taken to hospital on the walk today. Another two collapsed in the showers tonight. This is a seriously tough physical event.

The emotion on the walk today has been quite amazing. All along the route people were waiting outside their houses and businesses with hoses and ice to cool us down, cheering and clapping.

All the cars driving past honked their horns and waved too - many dressed up with Pink Ribbons.

Every time Janet and I went past one of the cheering stations we'd get all emotional again - really just an overwhelming feeling of community and love and support.

The dining tent was laid alongside a long fence that the walkers had to go along to get into the camp. All evening people stopped eating to cheer and wave to the last stragglers coming in.

When we got into camp tonight I pulled out the survivor T-shirt I bought before coming over, and I went to the Avon tent and bought one of the survivor caps they had.

Working my way up to wearing them on the walk tomorrow.

Day Two - April 20, 2002

Another huge day on the walk. Incredibly hot - over 30C (86F), not a cloud in the sky and the pavement was baking.

The girls from Florida are all starting to do it tough - especially Janet who just finished treatment in January. Mara started today with blisters so bad her entire feet were taped.

About half an hour along the road we saw the front page of the local newspaper - and there we all were, front page in a photograph on a story of the walk! The photo was taken at the opening ceremony when we were all crying.

At lunchtime I had to use my pocket knife to cut away the sides of Mara's shoes so she could continue to try to walk, but by the next pit stop she, Janet and Barbie all had to jump on the sweeper vans for a ride to the camp.

The walk this day was supposed to be 20.4 miles (32.8 km) - even longer than the day before. We heard tonight that there had been a problem when the organizers tried to set up the camp - they couldn't get power and had to move the site. This meant that it turned into a 26 mile (41.8 km) walk, with the last three miles (4.8 km) over rock - and I mean rock, not gravel.

By the time I staggered into camp at 5:30 p.m. I discovered the camping ground was also rock everywhere. We abandoned the designated camping site and headed for a spot by the water where the ground was not too bad and at least we had a view!

Too hot to wear the survivor T-shirt today but I worked up the guts to wear the hat.

Created a whole new set of experiences. One girl we had befriended said she was going to buy a survivor hat that night, and we said, "Oh, we didn't know you'd had breast cancer!"

She replied, "Oh, no, to show I survived the walk like you!" We had to explain that no, in fact I was wearing it because I was a breast cancer survivor - totally surprised and shocked her.

Had a better experience later in the day when things were really tough and was waiting to cross the lights with a group of girls. One was my age and was also wearing a survivor cap - made an instant connection and had a wonderful, affirming and happy exchange all in the time that it took for the lights to change.

I've never met so many other young women who've been through this experience that I could relate to. Starting to think things might have been easier if I'd met others I could talk to earlier.

Everyone else on the walk has been amazing too - an incredible mobile community - everyone says hello as they walk past and asks how you're doing - all genuinely connected. Really something special.

Day Three - April 21, 2002

Wow. Trying to come up with something different to say than, "What an amazing day." All of the emotion and effort reached an incredible crescendo today. Mara had her blisters lanced by the Paramedics last night, who told her not to walk today, but she insisted on giving it a go. None of us were traveling too well and Janet, Mara, Barbie and I formed a little group staggering along. We must have looked like we were at death's door because from the very beginning the sweeper vans were stopping next to us asking if we were OK.

When I first planned to do this walk, completing the whole distance was a big physical challenge that I wanted to attempt - trying to prove something to myself about being well now I suspect.

Today that really no longer mattered. Our little group was traveling so slowly I suspected that we wouldn't make it in time for the closing ceremony and we would be put on a bus - but really by then, making the whole distance on foot wasn't that important to me. Sticking with my friends and sharing the journey really seemed to be the point.

The distance on the final day was just 14 miles (22.5 km) - by the time we got to 10 (16.1 km), Barbie had headed off - we were walking too slow even for her, and Mara and I were slowing Janet down as well. The ambulances were loading people up at the Pit Stop to go to hospital and Mara and I decided the time had come to catch the bus. Janet opted to continue - we were concerned she wouldn't make it but there was no way we could keep walking with her so we let her go on her way.

The finish line was at the basketball stadium where you walked up the entry way stairs between lines of cheering spectators and participants who had finished earlier. It was incredibly emotional. Breast cancer survivors who were in the walk were wearing pink survivor caps and shirts - everyone who came up the stairs was crying, the spectators were cheering and crying.

After about half an hour Sue and Cindy came through. We kept checking the sweeper vans to see where Barbie and Janet were when to our utter amazement Barbie walked through the finish - she'd done all 14 miles on a cracked heel - this was the woman who had done no training and had never been camping before (and never will again!!).

By this stage we were really starting to worry about Janet when we finally saw her some distance away walking in by herself - she hadn't done more than 10 miles on any of the previous days, but did all 14 - the last four by herself.

We all ran out into the street to meet her - by this stage even the traffic cops were crying and weren't going to stop us! Janet and I made the victory walk up the steps together.

Inside the stadium we all got T-shirts for finishing the walk - breast cancer survivors got pink T-shirts, walkers got blue ones and the 230 volunteers on the walk got white ones.

While we were waiting for the closing ceremony we watched a video presentation of the walk - from start to finish - and there we all were again on screen as a group at the opening ceremony.

The closing ceremony was at a nearby park and it was arranged so that the volunteers would enter as a group, the walkers would enter as the group, and the breast cancer survivors would go as a group (which Janet and I weren't totally happy about because we wanted to stay with the girls).

Eventually all the volunteers were called out first and lined the one mile walk to the closing ceremony, and then the walkers who assembled on mass in front of the stadium. The last group called out were the survivors - it was incredible to walk outside and be at the top of the steps (there were about 200 of us) and look down on 3,000 other people in blue shirts who were waiting for you, and knowing what they had done over the last three days to help you.

When we came out all the walkers turned around and burst into applause - it was an incredibly emotional experience.

We then all took off in procession for the final mile. The feeling and conversation in the group of survivors was incredible. I'd had some great interactions with other individual survivors on the walk, but there as a group, and with so many young survivors around me it was even more amazing.

In the time it took to walk the mile we shared all sorts of stories - diagnosis, treatment, getting on with life after breast cancer. An amazingly powerful experience of community.

In front of the stage the walkers were split into two groups either side of the stage with a gap in the middle. The survivors were asked to wait and when everyone else was in place we ran, walked, limped and crawled down the middle - we found our girls half way along and broke out of the group - more hugs, more crying.

Once we reached the stage, two more survivors told their stories and again read the poem from the opening ceremony. The circle of survivors walked down the middle of the crowd again representing all the lives that had been lost, and we were reminded again that while we were walking, 245 women had died in the U.S. from the disease.

Then it was all over - we have arranged to meet the girls again tomorrow for lunch and a much needed drink (the walk was alcohol free).

All in all it has been a truly amazing experience - the event netted $1.8 million U.S. for breast cancer research and treatment, which is extraordinary in itself.

It's also been a really incredible experience for me personally. In the course of three days I have started to finally come to some acceptance of breast cancer as forming part of my identity. Also a really powerful experience of support and community.

Suspicious Lumps

When you get into a tight place
and everything goes against you,
till it seems as though you could not
hang on a minute longer,
never give up then, for that is just the place and
time that the tide will turn.

HARRIET BEECHER STOWE

From: Megan
Sent: Friday, January 17, 2003

In a chatty mood, so here it comes...

I loved your chronicles of the Avon Walk in Florida last year. Geez it sounds intense! Two days makes more sense - less dangerous, more accessible to more people, and all the same connection and fundraising benefits. Congratulations on participating. The insane flight must have been a big help also. I love the motorcycle shot. I forgot to tell you that I had been searching the web (to no avail) for a good Lara Croft on bike photo when your awesome photo with Dexter came through. Even better than what I'd been looking for!

I'm really glad you enjoyed the videos from our trip to Australia. It's fun to share, and unless you were there, they lack some of the pizzazz. I know it's cheating, but the bald head and sappy music guarantee tears for almost anyone that watches the triathlon, including me. I cut some of the best parts - Sharon ran like crazy to tape the whole thing, and there are whole sections of her huffing and puffing "I don't know, breath, breath, how she, breath, breath, is doing it." She didn't drink any water and was totally dehydrated by the end. She slept on the train ride back to Sydney, which I thought was wonderfully ironic.

I wanted to clarify a couple of things. One - I want full credit as the triathlon was a scant 34 days after my last chemo cocktail. Looking back, I know I am a nut case! Two - getting caught in pink. In my defense, I did a 5K "Race for the Cure" two days before we left for Australia. As usual, they hand out those pink shirts to survivors. Somehow it made it into my suitcase - possibly the only clean thing as we raced to the airport? Also, I only wore it to sleep in, never in public, and what you cannot see are the very butch Nautica boxer shorts that complete the en-semble and allow me to remain a respectable les-bian! I'd like to swear that I have no other pink shirts, but I do have a Ralph Lauren men's oxford that I adore.

I'm grateful for the role models that came my way when I was diagnosed. In particular, a friend of my Mom's that I have known since high school was diagnosed a month before me. She insisted I come over immediately to chat. She taught me to sit and talk about it calmly and rationally, and she set the example in terms of an incredibly positive attitude. She lost her other breast to cancer 10 years earlier.

I also talked to another friend of a friend who was told by an expert panel at Stanford that she basically had no hope. She continued training for a marathon through her chemo and is still around several years later.

Like you, I looked at my 35 years and decided I'd had a pretty amazing life. I have no intention of checking out any sooner than necessary, but if it ended today, I have no regrets and have managed to do more, experience more and enjoy more of life than most people who live twice as long. Gratefully, I came to that peace of mind the day I was diagnosed.

So, Sharon thinks she's found a suspicious lump in my remaining breast. I've decided to institute a "hands off the remaining boob" policy. I'll see my surgeon next week as a precaution. I cannot imagine it is anything - I don't think the chemo is even fully out of my system, and I saw my oncologist two weeks ago. I'm pretty pissed at the emotions that have shown up though. I despise being this vulnerable. I cannot even bear the thought of going through the whole thing again, even though I know I would step up and do whatever I needed to.

It does occur to me that I should have the other one removed so as to hopefully avoid these little scares over the next 50 years. I will have to admit that I have broken out the chocolate and wine (just when I'd finally lost the first 5 of 15 pounds I put on last year). My Lara Croft Tomb Raider DVD is playing in the background. There is such a fine line between moving on and having life put on hold. It sucks to have so little control.

Thanks for listening. The best thing about email is that you are always there.

From: Meredith
Sent: Friday, January 17, 2003

After all the scares I've had with lumps over the last two years I resolutely refuse to do any breast self examination. If John finds anything I've told him I don't want to know! I figure with a mammogram each year and 6 monthly check ups with the doctors they'll find anything significant if it's there and in the meantime ignorance is bliss. (I did mention denial is one of my favourite coping strategies!)

That being said I know exactly what you're going through - every time I find another lump or even if my health seems a bit out of sorts it scares the crap out of you. I think the reaction is probably so strong because we are still so close to having gone through chemo (even if it's 17 months since my last dose) - maybe it will get better as time goes on. It pisses me off too. The whole experience has made me more volatile emotionally than I used to be - that along with going off the pill means I am also back to PMSing in a big way! (Lucky John!)

I told you about my great secondary cancer of the belly button scare - I was just finishing radiation and was getting ready for my next lot of chemo. I actually had to fly to San Francisco for work two weeks after my next dose of chemo so to get my immune system up to speed I was having daily injections of Neupogen in my stomach. After two weeks of that it was as sore as hell and I was poking around and found a lump.

Because it was Easter I couldn't get in to see my doctors until the following week, and because my immune system was depressed they couldn't schedule the surgery for another couple of weeks until I got back from San Francisco. A really weird couple of weeks - a great trip and all, but with a bit of a cloud hanging over my head.

I had the same scare when I had my mammogram in September last year - they found more lumps in both breasts as well as my lymph nodes on the side I had surgery and I had to wait 24hrs to get the biopsy results - all new lumps, all benign or cysts. My surgeon who is pretty cool said that this was pretty much par for the course and would probably happen every time and to chill out about it (easy for him to say).

Each time it happens I think I'd rather just get rid of both boobs to get rid of all the drama - I know the research shows with all the treatment I've had the outcomes aren't a lot different with lumpectomy, but at least it would save all the worry.

My only suggestions in this situation are:

*   Remember that you are so close to finishing chemo that nothing bad could have survived that!

*   Get it checked out cause you'll worry until you do.

*   Self-medicate with as much champagne as you can lay your hands on.

*   Find a video game where you can shoot the crap out of something (Lara Croft - Tomb Raider II being a personal favorite).

*   Eat great food (because life is too short to drink cheap champagne and eat crap food).

*   Shopping for therapy - I bought an Armani tux in Nordstrom's in San Francisco on that trip!

Riding my motorbike is a good distraction too - you'll be able to do that soon! In the interests of solidarity I will hit the champagne and pasta tonight too (I'm just that kind of sacrificing gal)!

I won't tell anyone about your pink shirt if you don't tell anyone about mine. I only sleep in it too! It could be worse of course, you could have gotten married in the eighties. One day when you need a really big laugh I'll send you the photos. Think eighties big hair and a meringue for a wedding dress. If you haven't seen it, try to find a video of the Australian film "Muriel's Wedding" - all my sisters reckon it's the perfect model for what my wedding was like!

And yes, you're welcome to call anytime! Anytime that is, other than the middle of the night. The Avon Walk coaches kept calling me around 2:00 a.m. last year in the lead up to the walk and wondered why I wasn't very chatty!

Stay cool and think positive!

From: Megan
Sent: Tuesday, January 21, 2003

Thanks so much for your friendship and your great words of wisdom. They've been extremely helpful. I can't believe the number of scares you've been through. You are my "she-ro"!

I love the thought of shopping therapy. An Armani suit sounds awesome - any photos of that? If only I had a gala event to wear one to...

I made it to Seattle, following your prescription of self-medication and shooting the crap out of things.

Once I got here, I found a massive arcade. I bought the three hour unlimited use pass and shot the hell out of everything. I drove tanks and shot up everybody and I played Jurassic Park and shot all the dinosaurs and I flew airplanes and shot other airplanes and I machine gunned helicopters. I shot snipers and terrorists and zombies. I played all those games I am morally opposed to based on the unnecessary levels of violence. Then I drove all the motorcycles and race cars and wave runners. I am happy to report that I feel so much better.

It was a brisk mile walk each way from my hotel, and I am sure that helped. They had a great Harley Davidson simulated game. I rode it about 20 times. By the end, I was no longer running over all the pedestrians, and I rarely ran into solid obstructions. It gave me great hope for the real thing.

I hope everything is great on your side of the world! Enjoy some sun for me - it's cold here!

From: Meredith
Sent: January 21, 2003

Wahooo! Sounds like you're having much more fun than I am this afternoon.

I bought a Sony PlayStation 2 when I got diagnosed - I knew I was going to go nuts at home and that I really needed to kick something to get the frustration and anger out! Tomb Raider and Xena remain my favourites - not too gory and extremely satisfying to kick the butt of someone who really deserves it!

I'll have to have a scout for photos of the Armani - it is a suit to die for! I wheel it out for just about any function I think I can get away with it for. It is without a doubt my most extravagant purchase but it was one of those "what are you waiting for" and "what the heck" moments!

I always managed to justify having a top of the range laptop with DVD player (for those interstate flights), palm pilot, cell phone and digital voice recorder - she who dies with the most toys wins!

My best toy story was on my trip to India. Being technologically minded I had all of the above, my CD walkman, mp3 player, digital still camera and a video camera with me on the trip. All was well until the first night in the hotel after being on the road all day and needing to charge things up.

Plugged the laptop into the wall and all the lights went out. I thought we'd shorted out the whole hotel but it turned out to be only our room. Had the fuse replaced, plugged the laptop into a different power outlet, and shorted the room out again. In the end we could only use the shaving outlet in the bathroom to charge one thing at a time.

On our last day in India we were going to be stuck in the Bombay airport for 6 hours and I had been intending to work on stuff in the Qantas Club there - we had a running joke all trip that the way things were going we would get to the lounge, plug in the laptop and short out the airport. Almost, in fact - I shorted out the Qantas club and the entire lower floor of the airport. At that point I decided it was a sign I was not supposed to be working.

You made my day! You elicited the first genuine smile, that's for sure. I love the story of you blowing out all of India. Very Impressive!

I'm planning another trip to the arcade tomorrow morning before flying home and seeing my surgeon. I'm wondering why it is that anytime you really want to avoid the whole breast cancer thing, it shows up everywhere. The man next to me on the plane had to share his daughter in law's story (including tumors on her spine), my morning yogurt at the hotel has ads for the Race for the Cure, the athletic store has pink ribbons in the windows, and a woman in my nice safe real estate seminar shared how she has managed to do business while fighting stage IV, in liver and lymph, breast cancer.

I realize part of me thinks, "Do you have any idea what I have been through?" The other part recognizes that I have been through nothing compared to others, including you. Then I think - how warped I must be to compare the level of shittiness (does this translate to Aussie?) of one's experience compared to another's. I recognize that I continue to be hard on myself, even though this is supposed to be some-thing I am growing beyond.

Perhaps it is not a failure for me to be angry and scared and disoriented by this little scare, even if it is almost assuredly nothing. Maybe it is OK to be a bit depressed for a few days, and happy for the escape a drink provides. Maybe it does not undermine my general claim of an overall positive attitude.

I can't even identify the miserable emotions that seem to be coming to the surface. It seems to be more about my losses and suffering to date than fear about my future. I hate to admit that. I so hate being a whiner or complainer. So much for my positive, survivor attitude. But maybe I am not supposed to be perfect. If I even knew what that was...

From: Meredith
Sent: Tuesday, January 21, 2003

Buck up little camper - you're doing great!

I always tell people when you find yourself in this situation there is no right way to feel or behave, it is what it is, you feel how you feel, and you just do your best to cope.

Everything you're feeling and going through I go through too and I'm eighteen months and three visits with a psychologist further along than you. I'm certainly not above feeling sorry for myself.

I also developed a periodic pathological aversion to any cancer promotions - when I was first diagnosed, a cancer organization over here was running their big annual appeal and John had to buy me a Nerf ball to stop me throwing anything hard that was in reach at the TV. Not to mention that when you are bald or your hair is just coming back people tend to spot you for what you've been through and want to talk about their health scares which always seem insignificant compared to what you have had to put up with.

So in short - don't beat up on yourself for how you feel! Just do whatever you need to do to get by. Bad days come but they always go too.

From: Megan
Sent: Wednesday, January 22, 2003

As expected (or at least hoped), there is nothing wrong with me. Physically anyway. Just a little cyst that is of no apparent concern. Feels like a "gummi bear" rather than a "popcorn kernel", which I guess is good.

Amazingly enough, I feel like the weight of the world has been lifted from me. It is truly remarkable. I'm not sure what to make of the whole experience, and I am not looking forward to what it is going to take to lose the 10 pounds I likely put on in the past 5 days.

Lessons for this round:
* There is no "back to normal". I can't even comprehend the overall impact of this disease on my life.
* Alcohol serves an important function as a coping mechanism and a celebratory tool.
* You are truly a gift.
* I love video games!

I did have a good chat with my surgeon about her home search, so that is good news from the business side.

I knew you were going to be fine - I just didn't want to jinx you by saying so!

Great news - if not for the fact that I have to go do a training walk now I'd have a beer for you - will have to do that when I get back. You cannot possibly have put on 10 pounds in the last 5 days with all that nervous energy, not to mention leaping about the video arcade shooting things!

In relation to lessons learnt:

*   Normal is highly overrated anyway.
*   As one of the most famous Australian winemakers of all time said (and is still using in their advertising), "The one purpose of wine is to bring happiness!"
*   You are a gift too and you're welcome.
*   Enjoying shooting the crap out of things in video games is clearly healthy, good for you, and no indication of psychopathic tendencies.

I look at it this way - if anything goes wrong the annual mammogram will find it before any amount of poking around at my other checkups or in between so I try to limit stressing out to just once a year. In the meantime if it's there I don't want to know about it!

Therapy

I tore myself away from the safe comfort of certainties through my love for truth; and truth rewarded me.

SIMONE DE BEAUVOIR

Therapy:
Live Conversation - California, July 2003

Megan: Why did you eventually go to a therapist?

Meredith: It was about 18 months after my diagnosis. I was very volatile emotionally. I had never been like that before in my life. It wouldn't take a lot to set me off. I had this feeling of not coping when someone I knew relapsed, and being highly stressed about it.

And we didn't know how to handle this person's relapse with Dexter, so that was my excuse to go and see the psych.

We did actually have the conversation about how we should actually handle things with Dexter...about it all. Because Dexter had been so young when I got sick that we never...I mean Suzanne would have these God awful books on how to speak to children if their parents got cancer and it's like everybody dies in them! And I'm not giving this to Dexter. When I pointed out to Suzanne what was in the book, she didn't think it was appropriate to go there either.

So at my first appointment it was an interesting conversation about how the hardest thing for kids is when they don't get told anything. When they are old enough to understand and they don't get told anything, that's worse.

Megan: That's exactly right. And it's all about them. They think, "I did something bad".

Meredith: And why wasn't I told and all this sort of stuff. I'm not really looking forward to having that conversation with Dexter to be perfectly honest. But, anyway...

So, when I went back for my next appointment I was bloody stressed as all hell and I'm thinking, "Why am I stressed as all hell?" What was really upsetting me? I eventually brought it down to a couple of issues. One was that I couldn't cope about what would happen to John and Dexter if I wasn't there. And the other issue being resenting as all hell the fact that my mindset and my image of who I am and my immortality has changed. And that I'm not the same person any more.

So, after having worked all of that out in the 15 minute drive into the therapist, he said, "So, what are we talking about?" I said, "Well, I've worked out that these are the issues." And he said, "Yeah, you're right. So, this is what you should try to do about each of them." And that was my homework. And then I came over and did my first Avon Walk in Florida. And so that was kind of interesting.

The things that came out of that were accepting the fact that my overall view of myself has changed. I am not immortal. And that won't change. I have a different view of things. And it was right after that that I went on the walk. And I was actually not prepared to identify as a survivor for the first half of the walk. Not until the end of the second day was I prepared to do that.

Megan: So are you done with therapy at this point?

Meredith: Oh yeah. I didn't want to go back. I hated it with a passion. Well, we agreed that we had figured out what the issues were and that there were just things that I needed to either continue to work through or wait until enough time had passed that they didn't bug me so much anymore.

Megan: I only went for about 8 or 10 sessions. And you know, we had some really intense stuff going on at home. So it wasn't like I needed to go back and bring up the issues. They were right there every time I had chemo. And so it was more, "How do we work through this?" We were living it all the time.

I was pretty solid on the surface because I do the denial thing really well. And I do the heroic bit really well. And the stoic bit. And the stubborn bit. And so I could just power through. I seemed to have superhuman strength to get through the really hard stuff. This caught up with me later. Because I shouldn't have been able to do it. Kind of like the triathlon in Sydney. Physically, I should not have been able to do some of the stuff I did right after chemo.

Meredith: Well that was about proving that you're better or stronger than before. The other night when we talked through the chronology it was actually fairly similar for us as to when we lost the plot. Because I finished my chemo at the end of June and my whole life was supposed to be back on track. Before I got sick I was going to India and to London to speak at a conference. I had these things all lined up.

So I finished chemo in June and went to India, I had a trip planned in September to go to Greece and to Italy. Then when I got through that we were into Christmas and all the good stuff was going on for the holiday season.

When I got through that I actually had to go back to work, and cope and get on with stuff. Someone else I knew got sick at the same time and I completely lost the plot. You've got this plan while you are sick. These are the things I am going to do as soon as I am better. For you that was going to the Gay Games.

Megan: That's right. And being normal. Sailing and doing the triathlon and traveling. Just doing everything. Then we came back and the holidays were right there.

Meredith: They're a really good distraction, and you get through all of that and you feel better than you felt before.

Megan: And I had insane goals for the next year, including several long triathlons and a marathon and building a huge business. And what set me off was my knee going out two weeks into my post chemo training. So it was a physical limitation that made me realize, "Oh boy. This isn't really going to work." That triggered a complete emotional breakdown.

I was thinking that our emailing was unlike the therapist where you go once a week with sort of a script. Instead, I was able to put down my feelings, my thoughts, on an hourly basis without so much censoring.

Meredith: When you needed to.

Megan: When I needed to, yeah. And that is a totally different experience. I felt more exposed with you. We didn't run out of time at an hour. We "talked" about my issues as they came up, before I had my story worked out.

From: Megan
Sent: January 30, 2003

Saw my therapist today. I haven't done my grief work yet. Ugh! And my bum knee is my body crying out for nurturing. Hmmm. The recommendation is a weekend silent meditation retreat. Also, I am supposed to forgive my body for failing me. As I consider this extreme form of treatment, I'm having a piece of chocolate cake and searching the web for motorbikes. Feeling better already. I'm afraid she may be right, which is all the more reason for short term avoidance and distraction.

From: Meredith
Sent: January 30, 2003

My personal opinion is that going to therapy sucks, but it is good for you - honest! There must be a therapists' book on things to make breast cancer sufferers talk about - my psych asked me whether I blamed my body for letting me down or if I was to blame for getting sick - my immediate response was, "No!" Shit happens and it was just the luck of the draw.

Once I'd sat down and worked out what the emotions were that I was feeling - the whole grief and loss thing - and talked to him about it, he suggested that in addition to thinking about and accepting that, that I should think about what were the positive things that have come out of the experience.

As it happened I had to go away for a workshop over that weekend - at a lovely little town on the southern NSW coast, and there is this wonderful little isolated beach that I could go down to early in the morning and after the sessions were finished during the day.

I'd have to say there weren't a lot of positives that sprang to mind and it took some thinking, but in the end the things I settled on were first, the fact that when I looked back on my life I was really happy with the way I had lived it, and that I had a sense of fulfillment and pride in that.

The second was that I would never take for granted a single day or single experience that life would give me afterwards.

The last is that I have for most of my life tended to be fairly reserved in letting the people that I am close to know that I care about them. I take people at face value as I meet them and have never set boundaries on the emotional connections I make, but I have been hurt by people who haven't valued that or my friendship on occasions.

I decided after I got sick that life was too short not to tell people what they mean to you. After the walk in Florida last year I sent a long email to the women we met and walked with over there telling them what the walk meant for me and thanking them for being part of my journey, which I would never have done before. Kind of liberating really.

I find it hard to imagine that the person I was before this would have shared the things I have by email with you!

Ah well, a little introspection never hurt anyone.

From: Megan
Sent: Thursday, January 30, 2003

Just love the idea of emails passing in the night - or afternoon for you. I'll start with the "heavy" stuff and promise to end with the fun stuff.

I do believe in the importance of therapy, and I'm glad you've made some good progress down that path. I think us survivors probably all have to look at the same questions, although the timing of doing so and the answers we come up with will all be different.

I don't mind the chats with the therapist as much as recognizing and doing the "work" that comes out of those chats. Now that I am older and wiser (?) I have a sense of the pain and total letting go that goes with so called grief work.

It feels like approaching a black hole for me right this moment. I had a really difficult time when my grandmother died 11 years ago, and experienced a similar process when I came out in '94. I remember months of tears and alternately reaching out to people and pulling away.

I like the "good" you pulled out of your experience. I think they are probably even more meaningful to you since you had to struggle to identify them. A few thoughts (more for my own healing than trying to contribute additional insights for you):

1) Having a sense of pride and fulfilment at the way you have lived your life is something I think very few people ever achieve. Certainly not at your young age. It really must provide a sense of freedom to know that you are on the right track.

    I had a similar recognition of having no regrets at how I had lived my life when I was diagnosed. I consider that a great gift, especially since I can be so hard on myself in general. It was a big relief to know that I was OK with myself at least in a big picture context.

2)   I'm working on this one. I definitely have a new appreciation for the gift of each day. I give thanks and try not to take anything for granted. I'm guessing my rules around really being successful in this area involve some string of impossible to achieve conditions like never getting upset and always being perfect.

The reality is I don't look at life the same way, and I value more my decisions for today rather than always thinking of tomorrow. I would like to live even more in each moment and be able to really savour what I have right now. I met yet another woman who lost a partner to breast cancer. I suspect it is supposed to serve as my reminder to truly be grateful every day for all my blessings.

Maybe for now, I will just take the good lesson as you have so simply stated it and let go of the rest. And, maybe I am farther along than I give myself credit for. I know in the past, I would never have allowed myself the luxury and pure joy of sharing my thoughts through lengthy daily emails.

3)   This sounds like a huge breakthrough. There is something really comforting about being able to share your feelings with others. It does involve a bit of risk. I think most people are incredibly challenged when it comes to forming meaningful relationships. No one likes the feeling of being vulnerable, and we seem to spend most of our lives building emotional walls to protect ourselves from the experiences of life. When you are centered enough to share your feelings without needing a specific response, you are in a pretty amazing place. It

seems I get to experience more good stuff when I give of myself unconditionally. I do have to be careful since I have a tendency to take care of everyone else before I stop and consider my own needs.

I've always been shy about initiating conversations with people, and always pretty open and honest once they got going. It took a really long time for me to recognize that my idea of a friendship was very different from others'. Some painful lessons there, but worth it. I think we humans are designed to be closely connected with others and the happiness that brings is so worth the occasional bump.

OK - enough for one day. I am supposed to be "gentle" with myself and don't want to overdo it.

Bad Days

The cure for anything is salt water -
sweat, tears, or the sea.

ISAK DINESEN

From: Megan
Sent: Thursday, February 13, 2003

Warning - For mature audiences only. Contains explicit language and blasphemy. Uncensored by any positive thoughts.

I'm back from a run. It was definitely a good thing. I worked up enough of a sweat to cause the allergic reaction to my hair gel. I guess I'll have to learn to live with it because I refuse to shower before AND after every run.

The run was really cleansing in a self-flagellation kind of way (see, my advanced religious training did teach me something useful).

I'm going to dump the emotional crap into this email so:

a) it is captured for our book and I never have to consider recreating it;

b) you can read it, skim it or ignore it;

c) perhaps I will get some obscure, subconscious personal growth from the exercise (I can't help but do the sarcastic eye rolling at that one); and

d) we do not have to waste any time talking about it.

I doubt if I can recreate the same level of intensity as the shit that poured out of me while running. I got a full half hour in, but I did have to stop and walk periodically as the sobbing interfered with my breathing. It is almost as if your body can only take so much, and waves of emotion would over take me. I'd about keel over, then be OK, then more shit.

What is the deal? I am really sick of this. I do not want to be feeling like this. Unproductive, sad, angry, frustrated. I feel a lot of anger bubbling up. I do not do anger well at all. I have never really had a use for it. What do I do with it? Why is it necessary for me to experience it?

Like getting through the hell of the past 8 months isn't enough. Is this some sort of self-induced hell? What is the point? What is the purpose? I am not a bad person and I have not done anything wrong.

Why do I have to go through this? I'm willing to take on a whole bunch of life's crap. Why do I have to feel so f***ing miserable. Is the solution really to sit with it and write about it and accept it and move through it? What a lame, stupid process.

I should have known my idea of powering through all the steps in the grief process in a single drunken hysteria on the day of my diagnosis wasn't going to really work. If I'm way back on anger though, how the hell long is this going to take?

It so pisses me off to be limited in any way. I hate crying for no f***ing reason. What shit is going on in my head to cause it? I hate feeling limited in what I can do and be and accomplish. I can't focus for shit.

What am I supposed to do? Sit and meditate and be totally unproductive? For how long?

I'd chuck the f***ing computer out of the window if it wouldn't cut off my lifeline to you.

Where is all this stuff coming from? I really just don't get it. It's exhausting and distracting and depressing and overwhelming.

So what am I supposed to do? Sit here for a year and wait to feel better? Stuff it all back down where it came from and pretend everything is OK, knowing that would doom me to a life of feeling nothing.

So, my training says we now all know what Megan doesn't want. What do I want?

I want to feel OK to start. Like a whole person. Like a contributing member of something. Like I have some kind of value. I'd like to feel good and heaven forbid happy. I want to be done with the process. I don't want to process another f***ing thing.

Thanks for the ear and the never ending ability to make me smile no matter what.

From: Meredith
Sent: Thursday, February 13, 2003

Well the run must have accomplished a bit of catharsis...

Thought I'd put a few thoughts down to email to you, give you a chance to absorb and then call - we can talk about the tough stuff if you want or I can be a good superficial Gemini!

First off, no need for disclaimers or apologies when you have those days that you need to vent in an email to me - just go for it.

Not sure how many words of wisdom I can offer - yes it is sucky, yes I am going through it too, no I don't know why.

I do think my pysch put some perspective on it - when I finally caved in and went to see him it was because I couldn't put up with the crying jags and anger and all of the negativity which had never been part of my persona or life before.

We agreed that it was the symptom of some issues that I was repressing and refused to deal with and in the end distilled it down to two overwhelming emotions - anger and grief (with all the broader explanations that I gave in earlier emails).

What we also agreed that while acknowledging those were the issues and emotions was a start to moving on, it wasn't a quick fix - that the anger and the grief would always be there but as time went on the intensity would lessen.

I think I'll be really blunt from my perspective. Every morning when I get up and have a shower, I am reminded of the fact I had cancer - I mean the scar is pretty hard to ignore.

Half a dozen times through the day, particularly now that I am sitting at home where it is so damn hot and humid I am reminded because the skin where I had radiation itches like hell every time the temperature gets above 15C (60 F).

It makes it pretty hard to ignore the fact that it happened. And then on top of all that, no matter how positive you are about it, is the fact that my prognosis is 60% to get to 5 years.

That 5 year figure is a significant life post for me because I can't bring myself to make any long term plans after that. I'm stuck in an absolute instant gratification groove because always in the back of my mind is that something could go wrong and there is no point postponing things (hence my major funk about not going to Italy with my friend Kristen last year).

I do know that generally as time goes by I do better about all of this, although I do have relapses. Hang in there - I'm a year further down the track than you.

One more thought at the risk of poking in business I shouldn't interfere in - but I know that last year was even worse for me because work was truly awful.

I also know that as an introvert, while I love marketing and I am good at it, the sales/cold calling/selling yourself/telephoning stuff is really stressful for me and I hate it.

I was able to get to the position in my old job where I was mostly operating at a strategic level and didn't have to try so hard in those areas. So - do you think pushing yourself outside of your comfort zone with the phone calling and the real estate stuff is increasing your stress levels and making everything even more difficult?

OK - so drop a note when you are ready for me to call! PS - you realise that mostly the shit hits the fan for you emotionally right after you've seen your therapist - generally you're doing pretty damn good.

From: Megan
Sent: Thursday, February 13, 2003

You are amazingly insightful. Thanks for being so candid and blunt. Honestly, email feels a lot safer right now than the stupid phone. The f***ing tears have yet to abate, even after three hours.

You know, I have a pretty good case of denial going. Miss Engineer Megan has no idea what her odds of anything are. I know how many emails we've averaged per day and per month, and how many total pages of content we've generated, and the cost per minute of my phone card versus yours. I have no idea what my chances are supposed to be for recurrence or survival or a nervous breakdown.

I do know that I am having very strong live in the moment urges. I am having a very difficult time doing anything that smacks of being long term. I talk a good story, and I naturally think in terms of long term relationships and rewards and impact.

Right now, I just want to run around and be selfish and irresponsible. I wouldn't even hesitate if there wasn't this idea of earning a living. What if we do live long enough to run out of money? What fun will that be? Still, the thought of playing until it all runs out is there.

If money were no object, I'd fly down now and distract and harass you. I'd go full on to Italy this summer. We'd see everything in California while you are here.

We'd rent Harleys and really do the coastal route. For sure horseback riding next year. I'd do triathlons all over the world even if I sucked. I'd lie on the beach until I was sick of it. I'd work on our book without distraction - it's got to be worth something to someone.

Of course the pressure I've created for myself around real estate is unbearable. I refuse to do cold calls period. I can't even get myself to call my friends these days. People I love and care about and enjoy. Even when I give myself the OK to not even talk about real estate. I cannot bring myself to call them. It occurred to me today that a job at Starbucks would be a better fit right now.

But, I cannot bear the thought of giving up or quitting anything. I don't know how to not follow through on what I said I'd do. I feel like I should be able to do whatever I decide I'm going to do. Why is it so hard?

OK, I'm sending this one off while I continue to process.

From: Meredith
Sent: Thursday, February 13, 2003

All of that sounds pretty familiar, especially the plan to hire Harleys, kidnap you and take off for a couple of weeks on the great American road trip - don't think I haven't been thinking about it! Having to work for a living sucks. (Although I should point out that bikes are very fuel efficient and I am prepared to eat cheap junk food!) If not for John and Dex I think I would have sold everything and just taken off on the bike and around the world for as long as the money lasted.

The whole inability to focus on work and call people, even those you care about, is a textbook symptom of being stressed.

When I was diagnosed I couldn't bring myself to ring and talk to anyone - friends or family. Suzanne had to tell Mum and ring everyone else because I couldn't cope with anything more than me and John at the time.

I didn't even ring Kristen, although I love her to death and she is my closest friend - all I could do in the end was email her (what a chicken shit!) about a week after I got home from the hospital.

The moral of this story is that I also tell a good story and put on a game face but am a basket case a lot of the time too.

It was difficult for me to walk away from my job last year - I had 8 years of history there and I still loved the organisation and most of the people there. It just got so unbearable I couldn't stay.

Bursting into tears in two meetings about what was going on there and why I had to leave was kind of the icing on the cake.

I admit it did feel a bit like quitting, but you know in the end the price just wasn't worth it. Now I have some distance from the decision I think it was the right time to move on anyway - time to refocus in other directions - not quitting - strategic change of direction!

One more thought - despite the perfectionists we are, it is OK not to cope you know - not a sign of weakness or failure.

From: Megan
Sent: Thursday, February 13, 2003

The nasty stuff must have run its course for this round, because I now just feel exhausted and kind of spacey.

Sharon came home with roses and a sweet card. I just couldn't rise to the occasion, which sucks. She's off to a fundraising event. I'm glad to skip all the people, although the theme is chocolate. I'm not sure how to share what I'm experiencing with her. I can't even explain it to myself. "I feel like shit. I don't know why. I don't know how long it will last. I can't commit to anything. I can't contribute anything. I want to run away and hide. What do you think?" No wonder this experience ends so many relationships.

Funny, I bucked up enough while Sharon was here for the tears to stop. Now the faucet is back on. This is so ridiculous.

From: Meredith
Sent: Thursday, February 13, 2003

Well, I can't say that I really discuss this stuff with John at all (hence our apparent email addictiveness to chatting with each other). Sort of goes along the lines of, "I have ennui/am in a really shitty mood and suggest you go hide somewhere safe until it passes."

Given that this has also been a standard operating procedure for doses of PMS prior to breast cancer the system has been well road tested and works.

I am so good at putting on appearances that when I finally lost the plot and told John I thought I need to go see a psych he was genuinely surprised because he thought I had coped perfectly well and put it all behind me.

So, email and call when you want to.

Now that we have guidelines for emailing (i.e. as much as you want, when you want), we should have some good ones for phoning:

* Call whenever you want, but expect less inter action if it is in the middle of the night/early hours of the morning.
* Being both introverts and prone to long bouts of introspection it is OK to sit on the phone and not talk but just hang out in the quiet without feeling the compulsive need to fill the silence with chit chat.
* Calling to whinge/whine or cry is cool if we can overcome our introvert reserve on such topics.

Take care of yourself now!

From: Megan
Sent: Friday, February 14, 2003

You're the best. Thanks so much for being there with me throughout my meltdown. I never felt alone, and that is the greatest gift. It does mean a lot that I was eventually able to call. I am always here for you, so never hesitate to send an SOS.

We definitely set a record for time on the phone - we must be doing better in terms of being introverts - at least with each other!

I want to hear the minute the bike comes in. I forgot to mention that I have your picture on your bike with Dex printed as an 8x10 for inspiration. I pulled it out today for extra strength. I'll check on rentals for when you are here.

Today has been a great day. The beach was spectacular. The ocean is about 40 min from us, and I really need to go more often. An overcast day, but not too cold. Not a lot of people, although the freeways were packed. It's a three day weekend as we celebrate President's Day Monday (Lincoln and Washington are spotlighted).

There was tons of driftwood all over the beach - some pieces were complete trees. One was at least a meter in diameter. I found an abandoned fire and stoked it back to life. Something nurturing and healing about the whole thing.

So, I've processed a few things today, and thought I'd share my insights (the one's you warned me would show up and pop me) now that I am something other than hysterical.

The biggest thing that occurred to me today is the fact that I was diagnosed a mere 8 1/2 months ago. Yesterday I was really stuck on how long it was going to take to work through it all. It feels like it has already been forever and I should be done.

But 8 months is nothing, especially when so much of that was spent in shock and treatment and denial. So, I thought maybe I'd cut myself a small break and recognize that maybe I was expecting a wee bit much of myself in terms of instant recovery.

Thanks to all the groups and clubs and coaching things I'm involved with, I did about 8 goal setting workshops in December and January. I'm looking at my goals for the year right now and laughing.

Totally outrageous and unrealistic and would require a superhuman effort even if I had a fully functioning brain and body. The funniest part is I totally thought I could do it. Now I'm thinking maybe the half ironman tri, marathon and making a bazillion dollars may not be must haves for this year (along with a few others).

So, I am going to chuck the lot of them and start over with things that are important enough to focus on, and that will likely not kill me in pursuit of them. Learning to ride a motorcycle, completing the Avon Walk and finding a way to Italy are pretty good.

I suppose committing to continue with the anger/grieving/healing process might be of some long term value. And making enough to cover expenses this year would be really cool. Making huge progress on our book is a new one that I will definitely add.

I've been thinking a lot about how I can make adjustments to my career and day to day activities to cut back on the stress (most of which is self induced as you might have gathered).

Your comments hit home very clearly.

The reality is I can't do all of what I'm pretending I'll be able to do. Instead of feeling like a failure when I don't do it, I am going to change the expectations up front so I have less to worry about. We'll see how this plays out in real life.

I was really struck by my journals from 1994. It was kind of upsetting to recognize that I am going through the same process emotionally with the same feelings, although different circumstances, 8 years later. It seems that I am supposed to pay attention to this message (whatever it is) or I am destined to face it again and again. I'd like to at least get a new lesson to work on with the next big crisis!

I was looking at our email trail from yesterday, and I want to thank you again for your incredible insight and honesty, friendship and support. I gave you numerous opportunities in my somewhat flippant post run email to stick to the superficial if you'd chosen.

Instead, you created a safe place for me to go through the whole bloody thing in my own time and my own way. No small feat given the email format I restricted you to. I know you were just being you, and I want you to know I am truly grateful on so many levels.

Have a wonderful Saturday night. I'll be back soon!

From: Megan
Sent: Wednesday, February 26, 2003

I was thinking about my frustration over going through some of the same processing as in the past. I decided that maybe it isn't exactly the same, and wondered how I could give myself some credit if I really wanted to. I started thinking in terms of recovery time. Like when you work out after months on the couch and it takes you a week to recover enough to walk again. After you've been to the gym consistently for a while, your recovery time is a lot shorter.

That's what I decided about this emotional journey. I am farther along the path because my recovery time is much shorter, and I am able to get to the heart of things much more quickly and directly. I feel better thinking I've progressed a bit from 10 years ago!

From: Megan
Sent: Monday, March 03, 2003

I am noticing little sparks of excitement within myself, which is kind of cool. Finally! It has been so incredibly beneficial for me to be able to process and type away and share.

It is so amazing that you have taken the time to listen and respond with such intelligence, thoughtfulness, honesty, trust, compassion and genuine interest. I'm kind of flabbergasted, but mostly unbelievably grateful.

I'm feeling more and more that there is not something wrong with me and the way I think my way through things. It just is, and I really have to let it be OK and create the space for it.

I think I went along with the notion that it was a bad thing for a long time. Now I very clearly see the necessity of identifying, stating and insisting on whatever I need to feel whole and complete.

Check Ups

We all live in suspense,
from day to day
from hour to hour
in other words,
we are the hero
of our own story.

MARY McCARTHY

From: Megan
Sent: Thursday, April 17, 2003

Getting lots done, including icky stuff like scheduling
my check ups. Geez they seem to come up quickly.
Who devised the scheme in which we (the victims)
not only have to go to the appointment, but we also
have to be proactive about calling to set the appointment?

From: Meredith
Sent: Thursday, April 17, 2003

Ayup, check ups suck. At least now I'm only on 6
monthly check ups, and as you know, the only one
really worth stressing about is the annual mammogram,
because that's the only time they're going to find
anything.

From: Megan
Sent: Thursday, April 17, 2003

Of all the things to be thinking about at the gym, this is the email that stuck with me...

Since I had a mastectomy, there isn't anything to shove into the mammogram machine on the "bad" side. I'm not too worried about the other side. Worrying about it is like worrying about any other awful thing that could ever happen.

So, I'm thinking the only way they will find anything is when the doctor actually goes poking around the flat side (because I sure as hell am not going to do it). Not sure why this has captured so much of my attention the last couple of days. Just thinking about going to the doctor stirs it all up I guess.

From: Megan
Sent: Wednesday, May 7, 2003

Survived the day and am thinking an email cleansing and a good night's sleep will probably do me some good at this time of night.

Everything went fine with doctor. He asked me if I had experienced any nausea or vomiting. I told him only as a result of being in the building (which is normal of course). I was very restrained and did not tell him that I suspected he made me nauseous as well. I got the all clear (yeah!) and get to go back in another three months (ick).

At the end of the day, I'm wanting to vent for a moment if you don't mind.

As you know, going to the doctor is miserable. With all the recent personal development stuff, I kept thinking I should give the whole thing a new meaning. Like being grateful for being alive and healthy and talking about triathlons and fundraising walks and that my treatment was over rather than just beginning. I know I had the choice about what to think about.

So what thoughts did cross my mind. I felt nauseous, of course. That awful feeling stuck with me for a long time. I think it was a piece of bread I ate that finally settled it a bit. I actually started to cry while waiting to be seen. That really upset me. I thought if I was really advanced in my personal development, I would sit with those feelings and really work through them. F*** that. I really don't want any more of those emotions than absolutely necessary.

It's like going back to that office/chemo torture chamber instantly triggers 100 things. Fear and anger and resentment and vulnerability and sadness and uncertainty. I was surprised at how close to the surface and intense all of those emotions were. After "working through" stuff the past four months. What's up? I am sure time helps lessen the intensity of it all. Still I feel a bit of woe is me.

The other wonderful tid bit is that it is time for my mammogram, so I get to go back in three weeks. I decided that the trade off for starting this sick ritual 15 years earlier than I'd planned, is that I only have to be subjected to the flattening of one side rather than two. There had to be some benefit.

Other than the emotional stress of a stupid little visit to the doctor, the day went well. Some good meetings, talked with some great people, and my deals are on track to close Friday and Monday. Basically, life is good. I'm looking forward to tomorrow.

From: Meredith
Sent: Wednesday, May 07, 2003

Now sweetie, I know you've done a lot of excellent personal development work, but the reaction you get when you go to your hospital is nothing to do with any of that. It's a Pavlovian trained response - every time you were there, they made you sick, so physiologically you are trained to feel nauseous when you get there, as well as all the other emotions you were trained to experience at the same time. I get nauseous and nervous just driving past my hospital and note, it doesn't happen when I go to other hospitals!

I think this is going to be one of those "just is" things - it will probably go away eventually, and even if it doesn't, its basically a dumb ass animal instinct and doesn't mean zip - you aren't back sliding on your emotional growth!

I have to concur that mammograms are no fun. You are indeed lucky you only have to get one side done. Let me tell you, they are somewhat difficult if you aren't particularly blessed with cleavage - it's hard enough with the one full boob I've got left, but the 3/4 pounder on the other side gets put through torture to stick a worthwhile bit into the damn machine.

So, apart from all that, glad you had a good day!

Check Ups:
Live Conversation - California, October 2003

Meredith: The three month check ups have never particularly worried me, because although there is a level of stress there, they just poke around and I figure if it comes back, it will start small and the first time they'll pick it up will be in the annual mammogram.

Although, mind you, that might just be a really good case of being "openly in denial", because when I think about it when I have had the full on annual check up, which is when I really stress about it - the mammogram and the ultrasound, they've always found lumps there and they've been quite significant and they haven't been there the year before. So my cunning plan is possibly not all that valid, but I'm not going to think about that too much.

The first annual check up I had was after 10 months of treatment, and you know you get poked and prodded and checked out every week during treatment.

Certainly with radiation you are getting it every week, and with chemo every three weeks. So my treatment ended in June, and my first annual mammogram and check up was in September.

I was certainly really stressed going in. It was the week before John and I were going on our big trip to Italy and Greece. Which was kind of funny, because I really wanted to get it over with before we left, and if it had come back I would have just said, "Screw it!", and gotten on the plane anyway.

John said to me he didn't know why I'd scheduled it the week before!

Megan: He didn't want to know!

Meredith: Well, it would have been on my mind the whole time we were overseas, so I really wanted to get it over and done with. So that time when they did just the mammogram nothing showed up at all.

It wasn't a big deal. It was really stressful to go through, but at least I got the results the same day. The way they set it up is you get the mammogram and then take the films straight up to your doctor. And that was all cool.

The second year I went back, I'd booked it really late - a further example of being in denial about it. I couldn't get the mammogram and the doctor's appointment on the same day. It had to be the day after.

I went in for that mammogram at the hospital which I'd had chemo in, which was a bad choice because the place makes me nauseous.

I went in and had the mammogram, and then was told to go sit in the waiting room while they look at the films. Did that, and then they came out and said, "We'd like to have another shot at it, we're not sure we got a clear enough scan."

So I had to have the mammogram again, which was no more fun the second time around. And then got sent back out to wait about half an hour and then they came out and said, "We'd like to do an ultrasound."

And I'm thinking, "Oh...here we go..." Particularly since they hadn't done that the year before. Now I've discovered that they will routinely do ultrasounds because of my history.

But that's certainly not the way it was explained to me then. So my first thought was, "this is not the way it happened to me last year."

And so I'm lying there and they're doing the ultrasound and poking around the place and you know as soon as they start doing that locking on thing on the computer at a spot that they've found something.

So I said, "OK, what's happening, what's up here?" The technician said, "Oh nothing, this is just routine." I told her, "This is not routine, I've been here before, what's up?"

She said, "Oh there's just something we want to have another look at." Then they decided to do the fine needle biopsies again, which was seriously freaking me out.

Once again, they were saying it was all routine, and to me, it wasn't routine. It wasn't what was done last year. They didn't explain why it would be different this year.

The last time I'd had all this done was the time that I'd had cancer.

By the time they'd gotten through all that it was fairly late. You couldn't use your mobile phone in their waiting rooms, and I was desperately trying to ring John to tell him I'd been held up and why, and to get hold of my surgeon to say, "I'm being stuffed around here and is there any way I can get in to see you tonight with the scans?"

He wasn't available, but his secretary said the biopsy results would get sent to him in the morning anyway and they really wouldn't know anything until they got the results back.

I was really strung out and stressed, and rang John and Suzanne when I finally got out. I think we may have even arranged for Dexter to have a sleep over at mum and dad's that night because when things are really hitting the fan I don't want him around to see how stressed I am.

The next day, Suzanne took the day off as well, and we were hoping to get the results around 9 or 10 in the morning. The first time around my local doctor called me with the results first thing in the morning so I didn't have to wait.

But this time, although I have a great surgeon and get along with his secretary really well, he didn't call first thing in the morning when we expected.

I started calling her, and she was saying, "I think we'll have the results in the next hour." I was ringing every half hour trying to get the results out of her.

Then they finally turned up, but my surgeon wasn't around, so she couldn't give the damn results to me until even tually she caved in and said, "Look, you know I can't read the results, and you know I can't tell you anything, but there's nothing to worry about."

I finally got my surgeon on the phone and he didn't see it as such a big deal at all, and said, "It's all fine and you've got to expect that this is going to happen to you every year."

I'm like, "Thanks, I'm really looking forward to that."

Then we get to this year, and I went to a different hospital this time. I went to the hospital I had surgery at, because I figured going to the place I had chemo at was not a good idea.

I think I was relatively calm this time going in, because I expected to get put through the wringer, because it happened to me last time and it worked out OK last time.

It wasn't as scary this time around. So I went in and had the mammogram and got to sit in the waiting room. It had a fantastic display of brochures, including the one on the core biopsy, which I had to read because I knew that was the one that you got - and it sounded every bit as bad as you said it was.

And then went for the ultrasound - and they were good. They told me up front when I had the mammogram that they would do that routinely because of my history and because it gives a better image.

They did the ultrasound and while I was still lying there, the technician was poking around and obviously found some things because she was locking on to them with the machine.

And she was really good, she said, "Look, I've found this here, and this there, and they don't look like anything serious to me, but I'll get the doctor to have a look just in case."

Then she wanted me to poke the damn things so I knew where they were and wouldn't scare myself if I found them later, and I said, "I don't do breast self examination, so don't worry, because I don't want to know and I figure that's your job and you'll find them, and in the meantime I don't want to know."

She still made me anyway.

They were trying to find my old scans to see if they were the same lumps that I got stuck full of holes last year, and we couldn't find them. I thought with all the drama last year, they had been left at the other hospital.

In the end they let me go and said if I could find the old scans, and if they were the same lumps, then we won't bother, but if they're not then we'll have to do something.

I went up to see my surgeon and he had a poke around and wasn't really concerned about where they were. He didn't think they looked like anything, but said the same thing.

The even more annoying thing about this time was that I then spent two days trying to find the damn scans and couldn't, and then got to Friday afternoon and they said, well we'll have to go ahead and organize a biopsy. I couldn't get hold of my surgeon that afternoon to schedule an appointment, so I had to do it Monday morning and ended up with half an hour's notice to jump on my motorcycle and get in there and get it done.

They were really nice again. I went in for the ultrasound again and the doctor came in and had a poke around and said, "Well, I think we'll do a core biopsy!

And I thought, "Oh, great!" I actually had a good joke with him that it was due to my competitive nature because you'd only had one, and now I got to have two.

Megan: But you had the wussy one. You didn't get it done with a mammogram.

Meredith: No, that's because we're so advanced we can do it under ultrasound. I got to have it on both sides - one where I'd had my original cancer, and the other on the right side.

Megan: So you got to have two ice packs and then rode the bike home?

Meredith: That was very funny actually, because I was looking forward to the ice packs from your description, so they came in with them and I just shoved them down my bra and jumped on the bike, which was a really good look under the tight leather jacket.

Talk about being lopsided. And it was a bloody big hole - I've still got a scar there.

Megan: I've still got that scar too, even after the mastectomy.

Meredith: Oh great, so in addition to the surgery, and the four tattoos for radiation I'm now going to get another one on each side from these. Excellent.

What Causes Breast Cancer?

Be careful about reading health books.
You may die of a misprint.

MARK TWAIN

Work:
Live Conversation - California, October 2003

Meredith: I don't know that at the time I ever had a sense of something I had done or some cause for me getting cancer. It's interesting to me now that in our conversations about diagnosis, the first thing that I started with, quite naturally, was how hard I was working at the time.

The late hours I worked, and that I was really run down which I don't think at the time I consciously thought had an impact but it's something that has come up a couple of times since.

It must be sitting somewhere in the back of mind because it is influencing the choices I make now about how I work and what I do.

Every twelve months when I have the serious check up with the full mammogram and ultrasound, they find something else and I get stuck full of needles for biopsies.

The first time I went through all that was last year when I'd had the most appalling, stressful situation at work for months. I think even before that check up I'd been conscious of the stress and had the question in my mind of what is the impact of having to go through this work situation on my health.

I know it was certainly top of John's mind, and of my family's mind. I was training for the Avon Walk, which was also good stress relief, and Suzanne walked with me and we talked a lot about how unbearable my work situation was.

Suzanne just said to me, "Well, you've got to get out of there." Which I sort of knew, but there was also the stress of the financial implications of not having a salary.

Another big thing that was in my mind, because I talked to a few people about options for leaving and getting another job, was that I had no life insurance.

The only life insurance that I had was part of my company pension scheme, superannuation, and my coverage hadn't been effected by my diagnosis, but if I left, what was going to happen to that?

So that was another stressor for me in it.

When I actually went and had that check up and they found lumps again and I was waiting for the biopsy, I was incredibly worried about whether it possibly coming back was related to the work stress I'd put myself through.

And I had a real feeling of, "I'm a bloody idiot!"

I have a really strong memory of the day after I got the results. I'd taken that day off to drink lots and lots of champagne with Suzanne.

And the next day I was at work and the person there who had been making my life hell decided to rattle my cage again and called me up and wanted to know why I'd taken the day off.

I said I'd just had my annual check up and I'd been waiting for biopsy tests to come back and it wasn't a good space to be in at work, and this guy went into this long discussion about how he knew just what I was going through because he'd had a bit of scare with something a week ago.

I'm looking at this man and thinking, "You have no idea." Before diagnosis, at different times things went wrong with my health and I thought I was stressed then.

It was nothing like what I go through now. I've never felt so strongly the desire to lean across the table and pummel the guy.

That was a real trigger for me in making the decision to leave that job. I just had to find the right way to negotiate my exit and checking that my superannuation and life insurance would have been all right.

The stress thing was a big issue for me at the time. This time around with my annual check up, when yet again they found more lumps and scared the bejeesus out of me, it happened again at an interesting time.

Even though I'd had a year that was a hell of a lot better in terms of having time off, the three months before I had that check up, I had a contract where I was working two days a week interstate.

I was flying to Sydney every week, which was ridiculously tiring and I kept getting sick. I was thinking at the time that I shouldn't be doing this to myself, but also thinking, "Well, it's only three months and the money would be nice."

But my family, my sisters and John, were saying to me at the time that I should stop doing it and that I should just work part-time because I looked healthier and more relaxed when I did.

And it's really a stressor in my mind, and I know that it is in John's - working too hard and fear over what that would do to my health.

So I don't think there was anything else in my life that I would consider made me get sick. And I don't really know that working as hard as I did was what made me sick, but it still is a factor in my mind at some level.

Diet:
Live Conversation - California, October 2003

Meredith: When did you decide to become a vegan?

Megan: I went to a Tony Robbins seminar, because I am the seminar queen, in September 1993 - I was 26.

Mom went with a bunch of high school students. I had no idea who the guy was, but she needed an extra chaperone so I agreed to go. It was really random, really last minute.

They'd gotten a big sponsorship to take 30 kids to this weekend transformational seminar. And during the weekend, we actually did a fire walk over hot coals.

It turned out to be a really big weekend for me. I went not expecting anything and not thinking I needed anything in my life. What I got out of the weekend was a change in direction, and a feeling of independence - as an independent being.

I remember sitting in the bar with my Mom, having a chicken sandwich and drinking a beer during the break. And we knew the next part coming was the health piece.

I said, "I know what he's all about and there's no way I'm giving up any of this stuff!"

During the seminar, what I was really struck by was his energy. I was amazed that he could be on stage 20 hours a day and seemed to have unlimited energy.

Trust me, I was a big time meat eater at the time. I would come home from college and my parents would take me out for steak and we would go to Costco and I would load up on meat to take back to school with me.

So they had a full day of the health stuff and they talked about all kinds of things, including how to cure yourself of cancer or avoid getting it in the first place.

They introduced this Ten Day Challenge, and you know I'm just kind of built to take on a challenge. There were ten things to do for ten days and it just didn't sound that hard.

Some of the things I gave up were sugar, dairy, meat, alcohol and coffee. There were other things like breathing exercises and regular exercise. I couldn't argue that it sounded like a fairly healthy way to live.

I took it on, and I felt really great and I stuck with it. Well, not the no alcohol piece - I just did the ten days. Alcohol was something I never wanted to give up, but I made it through the ten days because I can be really stubborn when I want to.

So I lasted a full year as a vegan, maybe a year and a half. That was 1993.

And then I met Sharon...

Meredith: Meat eaters anonymous.

Megan: Yeah. I just didn't tell her I was a vegan at first. She didn't really know what it was and I just didn't tell her. She called and invited me out on our first date, and said she'd take care of all the food. I didn't tell her my restrictive diet, and she brought cheese, which was outside my veganism.

I loved cheese and it was the hardest thing for me to give up. And I really liked this person and wanted to spend time with her. So I dove right in. Cheese was the only thing I added for years and years. Eventually I went back to eating fish. It wasn't until after I was diagnosed that I started eating chicken, after 10 years without it. I had sincerely thought I would never eat chicken again.

When I was diagnosed, the feeling that came up for me was, "What the f***!?! What good did that diet do me?" What good did it do being a vegetarian for 10 years and a vegan for two or three years when really the whole point and motivation for me doing it was to not get cancer?

Meredith: Really?

Megan: It was definitely something I was conscious of. The extra energy was what got me to try it, and then the not getting cancer thing.

What happened was I started reading a whole lot of these nutrition books with all these studies, and "you won't get cancer".

And now I'm kind of angry about it because it didn't work. So, OK, what does work? If it's not the food, then is it the 23 years I ate anything I wanted, or is it because I kept drinking? Which piece of it was my fault? Which piece could I have controlled?

I was not good enough. And I realized I have always stressed about my diet. I am doing the right things, but am I doing it enough? Am I doing everything I can? Am I doing it right?

Meredith: So you obviously got really angry when you got cancer.

Megan: Yes I was angry!

I did the right thing and it didn't do me any good and also I must not have done it right.

And then I got diagnosed and I got the little nutrition booklet.

Meredith: I didn't get one of those.

Megan: I saved a copy, I'm happy to share it with you.

Meredith: No thanks!!!

Megan: Ice cream and macaroni cheese and whole milk. It's really designed for people who are on like chemo treatments for a long period of time and just can't keep stuff down. High fat and a lot of calories.

Meredith: You know this reminds me of how in sane I was at the time considering going into chemo as just like this great physical challenge or like "Survivor".

I was really pumped to see how well I could go through this challenge so be fore I even had my first chemo treatment I went to the supermarket and hit the health supplement aisle and bought all the health and training drinks because I thought I was going to be sick.

They taste disgusting - how do people drink that stuff anyway?? It was like I was going into this superhuman training regime and bought all of this crap health stuff.

Megan: Well my sister Shannon worked in a vitamin store at the time and she was even further down the vegetarian path. I don't think I've shown you the picture - she was about 15 years old and we are painting the kitchen. And she's painted "meat is murder" before we actually painted the wall.

She was a hard core vegetarian and vegan before me and she was really furious when I became a vegetarian because she'd been espousing it for 10 years and who was I to listen to Tony Robbins.

Meredith: Instead of listening to her first.

Megan   She was really upset. And she was veg-etarian less from a health standpoint and more from a protect the animals and the environment stance.

When I got sick, I went to Shannon and said, "What should I do?" I ended up with $300 of supplements, which I took with me to Montana.

And then when I got really sick from that crazy infection, I thought all those supplements did not protect me from my own stupidity!!! I decided I was not going to stress about taking all those nasty little drops.

Meredith: I don't think I went to that stage. I was just, ultra-prepared. I thought, "OK, you're on chemo, you won't be able to eat and you'll lose weight." What a lot of bullshit that was!!

So I bought all these healthy nutrition drinks which turned out to be a waste of time anyway.

The only thing I did take in terms of vitamins was I had always taken Vitamin B and multi-vitamins and then Suzanne told me there had been some trial done with Grapeseed to help with fatigue during radiation treatment. And it seemed to help. It should for what it costs.

Even being angry that your cancer beating diet didn't stop you getting cancer, you still haven't rushed out and started eating steak.

Megan: No. I'm eating more meat than I've eaten for the last 10 years though. As soon as I was diagnosed, I started eating chicken. I don't know if it was, "I'm just going to do what I feel like doing.", or something else.

There was definitely an element of, "This healthy eating didn't work."

So I slowly started adding back chicken, because I really felt like I wanted more protein. It was what I seemed to be craving. And sometimes you have cravings for things just because you are eating so much of them - like sugar, bread - you know the more you eat the more you want.

But when I'm craving chicken after not eating it for 10 years, I figured I must actually need the protein.

During chemo, I ate a whole bunch of macaroni and cheese and a whole lot of grilled cheese sandwiches. I got on a huge ice cream kick. I know it wasn't healthy. It was just making me feel better.

Meredith: Well at the time you're going through chemo you're feeling like such crap it's whatever you feel like eating. Like McDonalds - that's what I put my weight gain down to. I felt like I had a hangover, and that's what I eat then.

And I was supposed to get thin on chemo so I figured it didn't matter! Until after the first three months of chemo and I worked out how much weight I gained.

Megan: Yeah, I put on 15 pounds through chemo and I never actually lost any because I was eating comfort food and I never lost my appetite.

Family and Partners

*...and the time came when the risk it took to
remain in a tightly closed bud
became infinitely more painful than the
risk it took to blossom.*

ANAIS NIN

Partners:
Live Conversation - California, October 2003

Meredith: In all of the conversations we have had up to this point, you've mentioned that you went through a lot of turmoil with Sharon during the time you had chemo, and that's one of the reasons why you decided to see a therapist.

But you've never really talked in specifics about what it was that went on.

Megan: Sharon had a really hard time with me being sick. She jumped in when I was diagnosed and did a bunch of things. She was in charge and going to take care of stuff. She rose to the occasion and took care of me in the beginning.

She scheduled doctor's appointments and emptied my drainage tubes and those sorts of things.

But then...

I remember the first time I had chemo. She propped me up and then she left. I don't know if she went shopping or what she went off to do. And she brought me a cookie. Which is how I learnt that you don't eat what you like during chemo or you'll never eat it again.

It went OK, and that first night it was kind of anti-climatic - I was just hanging out and taking it easy. I felt better than I expected to feel. And then she went out again and I got the call saying I had to go back in because they got my dosage wrong.

I called her cell phone and I was really upset. Here I was doing this, "It's no big deal, I can be tough." And then I got that call and I just fell apart.

Sharon was fairly supportive, you know, "It'll all be OK." She took me the next day, and she was on top of them about doing it right because my biggest fear then was them giving me too much.

But then as things went along and I had the rest of my treatments things changed. Basically every time I had chemo she would get really upset and get really nasty with me.

We'd come home and she would start asking me, "When are you going to start selling houses?", and asking about the status of all my clients, and what my leads were, what calls had I made, who had I talked to.

The two middle treatments she got really upset and hysterical, and wanted to leave the house. One time she'd been drinking, and the other time she'd had Vicodin, and I didn't want her to leave, for a bunch of reasons.

First I didn't want her to hurt herself and I didn't think she should be driving, and secondly because I didn't want to be by myself. I had the sense if she left she wouldn't come back.

It was something really big for me, for her to actually leave.

Somehow I had more strength than I thought I should have, having just had chemo. I know it was actually the day I had chemo a couple of times.

We would have these big couple of hour fights where I would try to take the keys from her to stop her leaving, and I would try to rationalize with her, and tell her I'd work harder, and not let her leave.

I know we had one where we had a screaming fight out by the car and I was pounding on the car. I felt like I had to be as intense as she was for her to actually hear me.

Meredith: When you said she was hysterical, was she upset and crying or was she in a rage and angry?

Megan: She wasn't crying, she was furious. That I wasn't pulling my weight, that I wasn't working harder, that I wouldn't let her go. She just wanted to go stay somewhere else and I couldn't let her go.

I talked to my therapist a bunch about it - that's why I went in the first place.

It was really exhausting and upsetting. My therapist said, "Why didn't you just let her go?" If she wanted to leave that badly. But it's what I said earlier, I didn't want to be by myself, I couldn't call anybody.

It was really hard for me to call and ask for somebody else's help. I could've gone to stay with Shannon or Mom, but I couldn't actually picture myself leaving.

Although Sharon wanted to leave, I thought she'd be even more upset and angry if I tried to leave. And I didn't want anybody to know what was going on.

So I remember pounding on her car and getting hysterical, crying. If I got upset enough she would eventually calm down and come back and be normal again.

Then she would be really hungry and we'd have to go to Denny's to eat at midnight. I couldn't have possibly wanted to eat. Every time I remember thinking, "This is just insane."

Meredith: So you would get home from a chemo treatment, and spend hours with Sharon raging and being hysterical at you, and then be up and out all night?

Megan: Right. Then afterwards she'd be somewhat normal, although it was always touch and go. I never knew what mood she was going to be in.

I just wanted to lay around and watch TV, and we have a really small place. We only had one TV that had cable, so unless I wanted to climb up the ladder into our loft bed and watch movies - sometimes you just want to watch bad TV, not a movie - so I'd be in the living room.

But that's where Sharon's office is, and she works from home, so I'd be right there in her face and she'd just get nasty.

Sometimes she'd be OK, but sometimes I'd get dirty looks, or she'd make a snide comment or she'd turn the TV off.

I remember watching TV with headphones so I could just lay on the floor and hopefully she wouldn't notice that I was there.

One of the greatest gifts my therapist gave me was to say, "Why don't you get cable in the bedroom? No matter what it costs, at least you could have your own space."

It must have been the third chemo when Sharon went with me and took her whole office set up with her. Parked next to me there was a little nightstand and she set up her computer and got on her cell phone and started making business calls right next to me.

Chemo was stressful enough but there was just too much extra anxious energy around me. I wasn't going to say anything, I couldn't stick up for myself.

And I sort of had the mindset that if she was just there, she was supporting me and I couldn't tell her not to do that.

Meredith: Just turning up was supporting you, regardless of how she was acting at the time?

Megan: Right. Mom came that day, I don't know why. I think she may have had a sense of what was going on although we hadn't talked about it. So she came and got Sharon to go away.

She knew it wasn't OK that Sharon was acting so...it was kind of this aggressive business mode, you know?

Then the last chemo was the best be cause Sharon went to a seminar in L.A. without me and I spent the next 4 days by myself, which was great because I didn't have to do anything, or pretend to be OK. I could just worry about myself.

I watched TV and slept most of the time.

I don't remember Sharon actually cooking for me or taking care of me through any of it. Maybe once or twice, but it wasn't a consistent thing, I had to take care of myself.

So she came back from her 4 days in L.A. and I was just at the point where you start feeling better. She came back really excited, kind of super energetic about all the ways she was going to make money.

She wanted to do something special for me to celebrate the end of chemo so we went and stayed at this fancy bed and breakfast. It was nice, and I kind of had mixed feelings because I didn't feel that great and would have been happy to stay home.

But it was a sweet gesture and kind of nice to get out of the house and do something different.

Meredith: So looking back on that now, what's your perspective of your experience going through chemo?

Megan: My experience now is…that I was robbed. I didn't get a chance to be sick. It wasn't OK for me to be sick. It's a stupid thing to say I missed out on…but I wish I could have just laid around without feeling guilty and upset.

I had clients, and I was trying to sell houses and but at the same time I was so sick I really just didn't want to do anything. It didn't really matter. What ever my experience was at the time it wasn't OK with Sharon.

I feel like I went through it alone, and it would have been easier to go through it all alone in some ways. If I could have just been alone and miserable instead of all of those external pressures and feel ing really anxious all the time.

Not knowing what I should do or how I was supposed to react. All the time Sharon had an edge, kind of nasty and hard to be around. I always felt like I was somehow wrong. That I was hurting her by being sick.

I really just wanted someone to take care of me. And I knew she had limited capac- ity for that from past experience. She could be really great for a day, but if I ever got sick with a cold there was a two day maximum before she would get angry. I think that was in the back of my mind, that it's not OK for me to be sick. So this was something that had always been there in the relationship, but breast cancer really intensified it.

Some things that happened were things I never expected. She was upset more often, and it was nastier, and directed more at me. Any of life's upsets at that time were always indirectly my fault.

Some of that had been there before, but this was the first time it was so extreme and everything was directed at me, directly my fault. She was saying I was lazy, and why didn't I get up and go do something, and all I do is just lay around.

Meredith: What else are you supposed to do when you're having chemo? That's not OK, that's not alright for that to be thrown at you.

So have you talked to Sharon since that time about what went on?

Megan: No. Part of me doesn't want to go back and relive all of that - I mean it's in the past now. Plus I'm still kinda scared of what her reaction will be. I guess we have to talk about it some time or it's always going to be there in the background.

From: Megan
Sent: Saturday, November 08, 2003

My seminar was actually pretty good tonight. I didn't care that I hadn't done my homework. I got upset with my group leader about having a breast cancer conversation with Sharon since she kept following me around telling me I wasn't being vulnerable. Really funny to look back on, but I was not happy. I actually had a breakthrough thanks to all my good work with you the past couple of days along with the structure of the evening.

We are supposed to be practicing presenting material to a small group. Part of it involves a personal share. Like something from your life that you are working on and that is important to you.

I was working on something lame about not exercising, and my group leader was pushing me to work on the Sharon issue. So I grabbed Sharon and told her that my leader really thought we needed to talk about breast cancer and that I wasn't being vulnerable, ha ha. She actually agreed, much to my horror. Not sure if I was more horrified at her wanting to talk about it or my group leader being right. We also started a conversation about me protecting her and treating her like a kid.

I saw that I do treat Sharon like a kid. I don't trust her to work things out for herself. And I withhold how I am really feeling and what is really going on in order to try and protect her, and me. And I am left sad and scared and anxious. And we have a screwed up relationship that will not make it.

So I made up something new. The possibility of being trusting and free. Trusting of Sharon to be a grown up and look at what she needs to when she needs to. And free to be completely Megan - whatever the consequences. If that is really there, my life really will be transformed.

Still a little apprehensive about it. I shared with Sharon, and she seems ready to take it on. I told her I specifically was not going to chase her and try and fix things. That I would keep loving her without withholding, but that I might need to leave as she worked things out, and that I was not going to buy into things that weren't true for me.

I don't want to pretend all will be easy and well. But I also can't shut down trying to protect myself. I did tell Sharon I thought she had deeper issues that triggered her upsets and that I wanted to support her in honestly looking at them. I'm still tiptoeing around a little, but I said way more tonight than I thought I was going to work myself up to over the next week.

From: Megan
Sent: Saturday, November 08, 2003

I don't think I am supposed to try and resolve Sharon's issues, but she feels like we can't talk about it. I think I shut off the area since she gets so upset. She doesn't think she has a lot to say. I know the issue is deeper for her, but I can at least open the door and see what is there. So, no particular agenda, just letting it be OK for us to talk about it. Probably need to let it be OK for her to be scared of losing me too (in a grown up kind of way).

Once I muster up the courage to get us going, I suspect we will have some great conversations over the next week in Maui.

So good to talk to you today. First time I've actually called from a seminar I think. Totally perfect and cool. Definitely want you getting the blow by blow of my transformation! Actually, this stuff only works in conversation, and every time we get something powerful, they want us to immediately go and share with the people in our world. Otherwise it disappears. Can you believe they are claiming what goes on in our heads does not actually exist in the world?

I forgot to tell you that I did the very thing we hate. I accosted the poor leader at the first break after sharing with us that she was recently diagnosed with breast cancer. Before you put me in the lame category and refuse to publish with me, let me explain my rationale. I really felt compelled to say something given all the stuff that has come up in the past two weeks. Our conversations, conversations with Sharon, my group leader insisting I talk to Sharon. It just seemed like more than a coincidence.

And, I did not tell her my life story or pretend to be interested in hers. I said, "I was diagnosed last June and had a mastectomy (I only threw that in because she had a double mastectomy). I believe I'm in this course with you as the leader for a reason. Thanks for being here. (She's got reconstruction scheduled Tuesday). I have some unresolved issues around the experience with my partner and I withhold from her because I don't think she can handle talking about it."

She thanked me, and I was free to pay attention without all that running through my head the next 12 hours. I know there are additional issues and it is not all me or my responsibility. And, I've got to start treating Sharon like a capable adult, which means no longer withholding things that I think might upset her.

Also forgot to tell you my big insight for the morning. This leader has been doing this work since 1982. And she got breast cancer. Blows my theory that it is emotionally based. She should have been pretty transformed leading the courses for 20 years. Back to your argument - no one has a f***ing clue what causes it.

From: Megan
Sent: Sunday, November 16 2003

All is good here in Maui. I managed a couple of hours on the beach. The weather is still not great, but it was warm and gorgeous. The water is spectacular, and I got in and floated around for a bit. Really just taking it easy. I love it here. It is so relaxing - a special place for Sharon and me.

I had a good insight on the beach. I was talking to you in my head, as I so often do. I was thinking about something I noticed in what you'd written that you were maybe avoiding dealing with. Then I had a flash of insight around the issue I've been avoiding and was not nearly so happy about it.

I realized, much to my horror, that you are being incredibly honest and pushing yourself to the limit in terms of writing/talking about things that you've barely worked out. And I am being a coward around my relationship with Sharon. I need to write honestly about my experience of her through breast cancer. For me. And, I need to share that with her. And, it needs to go in the book. I cannot run around sharing this book with people if it has a big fat omission. And

Sharon and I cannot have an honest relationship with this unaddressed issue between us.

I don't know about the timing of that. Just want you to know that is the direction I am heading.

From: Megan
Sent: Monday, November 17, 2003

Enough thinking already! Really concerned about being able to adequately articulate. Doing my usual wanting to have everything figured out before going out on a limb. Just going to dive in with stream on consciousness. Then run away to the beach and let you ponder.

Definitely concerned about talking with Sharon about her behavior during chemo. Obviously I am concerned about her getting upset, although she has been unbelievable this week about staying in difficult conversations. So, I am less concerned about her getting angry and acting irrationally, and more wanting to avoid bringing up feelings of hurt and guilt and sadness.

I know we will both feel better after we get through the conversation. You know me, as soon as I figure something out or know what I need to do, I kind of obsess about it until it is resolved. It is a huge wall between us, and it was one thing when I was simply in denial. Now that I am openly in denial, it is an unbearable wall.

I've been thinking about what I want to say to her, thinking about a powerful approach to communication in which I take responsibility somehow. Not like it was my fault.

It ties in with my recent insight that I have shared with her - that I was treating her like a two-year old. Not trusting that she could work things out. If I had let her go run away and be upset the first time she tried instead of fighting and hanging on so tightly, she might have worked through all the emotions that came along with me being sick a little better. Letting her go when she wanted to leave was what my two months of therapy was all about. Just now getting to the point of doing that, 15 months later.

Even now, I am avoiding talking to her because I'm afraid she won't be able to deal with it.

I can see that I cannot direct how the conversation will go, and that it is impossible for me to work it out ahead of time. I had visions of working it all out for the book and giving it to her to read. Obviously, that is a lame idea.

The current plan is to talk to Sharon while we are here. I'll find the right moment. I had a good one yesterday, but I wasn't ready.

From: Megan
Sent: Tuesday, November 18, 2003

I finally had the breast cancer conversation with Sharon. She shared with me that she had this fear that she had actually caused my cancer by sometimes thinking about us not being together. Extreme pain and guilt for her. And, she was feeling "bad" because only a bad person could have said and done the things she did when I was sick.

I'm not thinking about it for a bit. Consciously processing is not going to help. Suffice it to say, it is a huge relief for both of us to have it all in the open. And, it feels like we really can talk about anything as it comes up, having dealt with the worst. I was so terrified I could hardly get anything out of my mouth.

From: Meredith
Sent: Sunday, January 04, 2004

Wow. Just finished reading your collection of emails on your relationship with Sharon. Absolutely blown away not only by your courage in being prepared to lay it all out there in public, but also what you went through in opening that all up again with Sharon by having the conversation instead of just leaving it all in the past.

I guess I had been peripherally aware that you and Sharon had a really difficult time going through chemo, and I was also aware that the whole breast cancer experience was continuing to impact on your relationship. Often when we were talking or emailing you would make some vague comment about it, but never any specifics, and although I wondered exactly what you had been dealing with, I never really felt I should ask because it was obviously something really painful and private for you and I wasn't sure myself that there was any point in dragging it all out again.

That day at Hermosa Beach last October it just seemed inevitable that it would come up.

One of those topics that we danced around for months I think! And so as a result of that, I've never really talked to you about what it was like for John and me, and a lot of that was a conscious decision on my part.

So much of the time we have spent together we have been talking through the whole cancer experience. And the impact on your relationship with Sharon has been so obvious and so painful for you. And my experience was completely different. To be honest it just seemed to me to be plain insensitive to be talking about how fantastic John was and how much closer we became through my treatment when things had obviously been and were continuing to be really difficult for you.

So in the interests of completeness, what was my experience of John through breast cancer?

I know that I was absolutely blessed in meeting and falling in love with such an incredible man when I was just a kid really - I was 18 when we met, got married just after I turned 20, and we had been together for 14 years by the time I was diagnosed.

In our whole life together, I can only remember two times when we ever got really angry in an argument with each other. I can't even remember what the first one was about - it was not long after we were married I think and I was just furious and went shopping for an hour to calm down. The other was when I was building a new boat and attempting to "hammer" fit a recalcitrant piece of rigging. John was quite rightly a bit agitated about me hurling a hammer at a brand new boat and got so angry he kicked a stump. Not terribly dramatic and we both got over it within a hour or two.

That's not to say that we don't bicker, and get cross with each other, and God knows when I am PMSing I am not a rational, pleasant person to live with. But John is amazingly calm and even tempered, and just waits for me to become rational again and everything is fine.

John was absolutely amazing throughout my treatment. Ten months was a hell of a long time to go through chemo and radio, and it took many more months after that to start to get my strength and stamina back. The only issues that ever came up were really probably due to my lack of communication about what was hardest for me.

I think just after we were told about all the treatment I was going to have to go through, John came to me and said he thought he should quit his job and just do a bit of part-time consultancy from home so he could look after me, which was incredibly sweet of him but got a tearful panic attack from me, because my biggest concern at that time was how would we cope financially, and John's full time salary was really important to me to keep going.

I never really talked through my fears and the whole emotional impact cancer had on me. I think John bought the whole stoic, "this is just a minor setback" routine I was selling everyone, so when I finally caved in and admitted to him that I wasn't coping and needed to go see a therapist, he was surprised but really supportive. And the conversations we had to have out of that were really difficult, but he was absolutely sweet and understanding and great through them all too.

I'd heard the horror stories of how badly some women's partners react in this situation. I remember while I was actually having treatment driving to work one day and the radio station I was listening to was asking people to ring in and tell horror stories about their ex-wives/husbands/partners.

One woman rang in to say she had two small children and when she was diagnosed with breast cancer she went home and told her husband and his first question was how long did she have to live in the worst case scenario. She told him and asked why he wanted to know, and he said he wanted to know how long he had to find another wife to look after the kids! Needless to say she ditched him, kept the kids and is well now and getting on with life.

I never had any fear about John not supporting me through my breast cancer experience. I did have some concerns about how he would react to the physical side effects like the surgery and the chemo, not from anything I knew about John, but your self image does take a beating when one of your significant assets gets hacked about, and when you then spend the next 12 months with no hair, eyebrows or eyelashes and looking like crap, it's hard to feel particularly attractive.

A few days after I came home from surgery the dressing was ready to come off and I asked John if he wanted to have a look at the scar, and I think his reaction was something of a panicked, "No Way!" I conned him into it after 10 minutes or so and he just said, "Hey, that's not bad - I was expecting much worse," and that side of it has never been an issue for him at all.

There was never a time through all the treatment that followed and everything since that he has made me feel any less attractive or desirable as I was to him before, and certainly our physical relationship through all that time was as active and robust as my energy levels were up for.

(OOOOOOOO - here comes the sex chapter!!!!!!!!!!!!!!!!)

I know I have related to you the disastrous impact of small children in a house without a lock on the bedroom door on parent's sex lives. Child free home days have always been very popular in this household!

Every time I had a chemo treatment, John would take two to three days off work and sit with me through the treatment and then stay home with me to take care of me for the next few days. The first time we went in I think we also arranged for Dexter to have a sleepover that night, because if I got really sick we didn't want him to have to be there for all the drama.

So we went and had the treatment, and I think I was totally pumped and I was in good physical shape that first time too, and the anti-nausea drugs were so great that when I got home I was feeling terrific. We had McDonalds for lunch, John worked for an hour or so and we just looked at each other and he said "How do you feel?" and I said "Terrific! Let's go to bed!" I know, too much information for you but it's a damn good story, and one that I haven't told anyone else.

John was also great about picking up more of the domestic duties while I was sick - he's always taken on a lot of the household chores, but pretty much he did all the cooking for a year while I was sick, and certainly a lot more of taking care of Dexter than I was able to. He pretty much gave up sailing for a whole year, despite having a new boat, because he wanted to spend all his free time at home with me and Dex.

He was also brilliant about not putting limitations on anything I wanted to do. It must have been hard for him to watch me fly off to Papua New Guinea, and India and America knowing how sick I was at the time, or getting my motorbike license. He was absolutely supportive of anything I wanted to do.

I remember when I had my first big check up scare I had a new bigger and much more expensive motorbike on order, and while we were waiting on the biopsy results I had second thoughts and started to worry again about our finances and said to John that I had decided to cancel the order if it turned out the cancer had come back. He just said, "Why? Go ahead and get the bike anyway."

I can't imagine how I would have coped with going through it all without him.

I think if anything the major impact of my breast cancer on our relationship has been to bring us closer, or at least to make us realize how to treasure and make the most of what we have. Living life fully, making the most of every day, and most of every minute that we have together.

From: Megan
Sent: Monday, February 17, 2003

So, Ms Anything-Goes... I'm curious how Dexter did when you were sick. Seems he's old enough to have known something was up. What did you tell him? How's he coping now? My niece Iman knew I had an "owie" and got a kick out of my bald head, but she was basically a clueless two year old. It must have been a lot tougher for a bright 7 year old.

Dexter was pretty cute through the whole chemo thing. I got sick just before he turned 7, so he was a bit young to really comprehend. He knew I was sick and when I was laid up in bed he would periodically troop in with a tea towel over his arm, snap to attention and ask if there was anything he could get for me.

I did warn him about my hair falling out and we turned it into a big joke. The day I got the number one all over he came home and was in hysterics - he kept running his hand over my head going, "Oh God! Oh God." Very funny! We never discussed the word "cancer" in front of him. He did visit me in hospital and knew I'd had an operation to get something fixed, but that was it.

He was actually over at mum's the day I got diagnosed, so he stayed for a sleepover for a couple of days - I visited him before I went to hospital and delivered a stack of new toys so I think he was happily pre-occupied.

The interesting thing is that although we never discussed it with him, being a smart kid he worked out that I had cancer. He'll sit in front of the TV now playing with his Lego and if a story comes on about some new cancer cure, he'll stop and turn to me and say, "Mum did you hear about that? They have a new cancer cure."

Generally I think he seems pretty relaxed about it all, particularly now I am well.

Family:
Live Conversation - Las Vegas, October 2003

Meredith: Suzanne always said that denial is a really powerful short term coping strategy, it's just that at some point down the track it doesn't paper over the cracks so well.

When I spoke to my therapist we agreed that it was never going to be OK thinking about dying, I am never going to be quite sanguine about it.

As time goes on, it becomes less of an immediate reality and it doesn't weigh in on me and trigger so much.

Although, you know, three years down the track I can't go and sit through "Finding Nemo". So now I'm "openly in denial" which is I think the point my therapist was getting to.

It was a really good short term strategy but I didn't know what the problem was and what was triggering me back then, everything was setting me off and I didn't understand why.

It wasn't until I actually sat down and confronted the issues and acknowledged them that it started to get better. After that, I can still go back to being in denial to some extent.

The only things that really trigger me now are those that I can see and recognise as being related to my situation.

Megan: Like a Disney cartoon movie? Why did "Finding Nemo" upset you?

Meredith: You remember that email when you asked me how I coped with Dexter through all of this, really asking me how I coped as a mother with breast cancer, and I skillfully avoided it by talking about how Dexter coped?

I guess the "Finding Nemo" thing is that although I talked through this issue with my therapist, seeing the first 5 minutes of that movie just brought it all back up again.

So, what's it like to be the mother of a 7 year old and be diagnosed with breast cancer?

It's really tough. There's all the worry over how my family will cope without me, and there was some initial stress over our financial situation.

I didn't have life insurance - well I certainly didn't have a policy. Which I should have done something about before, especially since someone else we knew who was close to our family and the same age as me had been diagnosed with cancer a few years before. If there was ever a hint to do something about it, that would have been it.

You never think it will happen to you. And John and I had a will made up when we had Dexter and had that sorted out and covered for guardianship should something happen to both of us.

But you never really think about what that would actually be like. It's the sensible thing to do, but why would you think about taking out life insurance if you're young and healthy?

The really hard bit about all of it is imagining my family going on without me. Initially it was more about the financial stress, but we had mortgage insurance so that if I died our mortgage would be paid out so that was OK, but raising a child is not cheap.

Then there was the longer term financial stability stuff. I did manage to track back through the paperwork with my company pension scheme - we have compulsory superannuation schemes in Australia where your employer has to make contributions, and as part of that it turned out I actually had some life insurance.

So I've kept that up since I've left my job because I'll never get insured again.

The financial situation, then, was a stress for maybe a week and then it was just getting through treatment.

Megan: So was that the main thought initially, how they would cope financially without you?

Meredith: Well it was a lot easier than thinking about the emotional and psychological side of it.

In talking to my therapist, I realized that really a lot of it has been projection on my part. We talked about John and his life and all the challenges he's been through, and John's very resilient.

So I got to the point where I could accept that John would cope, he would go on.

Dexter and he are very close. They would go on and manage together.

And it wouldn't be the same. But they would be OK. But that's still really hard to deal with for me.

It's a hard thing as a mother to think about the possibility of your son growing up without you.

I've never particularly been worried about the thought of John finding someone else. I would want him to do that so he wasn't alone. The thought of potentially someone else raising my son and being his mother doesn't particularly worry me, I just want to know that they will be OK.

So, "Finding Nemo" was a great joy to go see because the hardest thing for me emotionally is still the thought of my family going on without me.

John and Dexter and I went to see it, and Dexter gets a little anxious in movies sometimes because it's big and dark and noisy and a little overwhelming for him.

So the way we go watching movies is that Dexter lasts about three minutes sitting in his own seat and then ends up sitting in my lap. Which works for me, and I'm sure Dexter thinks it's a lot more fun too.

I don't think he even made it through the promos for upcoming features this time before he ended up in my lap.

And we get into "Finding Nemo" which starts fairly laid back, idyllic and everything else, and then the barracuda turns up and the mother makes the choice that she does, and the father fish Marlin wakes up and discovers his wife is gone along with all the other baby fish except for his son.

Dexter was just scared of the barracuda thing, so he's got his hands over his ears and I've got my hands over his eyes while he's waiting for me to tell him it's OK and he can actually look again.

And I'm sitting behind him bawling through the whole damn thing. Dexter's completely oblivious to the fact his mother's a basket case.

I could pull it together enough to get through and enjoy the rest of the movie but I was really raw about it. We went home and then needed to sort out lunch so I think I went out and got McDonalds and was still really upset in the car but needed to get away for a bit because I did not want to be a basket case at home.

I mean, I can't even go to see a f***ing Disney movie.

I thought I needed to get out and get my head back in order.

Megan: Is that your first reaction, to want to get off and be on your own?

Meredith: Yeah, it's still about not wanting to do that in front of them and have them put up with my crap. And I thought it was just an immediate reaction and that I'd get over it, but I was still a bit stuck by the time I got home.

So I went into my office at home to finish off some work and John came in and saw that I was upset and I explained to him why, which he understood but the movie hadn't had the same effect on him. He hadn't identified with it at all.

It's just the recognition factor, I see that and it takes me back to where I was. I see myself in that situation and it's still really raw.

It's an issue that's always going to be there, it's always going to be part of it for me. It's not front and centre as long as I'm healthy and life is going on, it's not something I fret about on a daily basis.

There are no guarantees in life anyway. It's not just cancer, anything can happen. It's just that having been sick it makes it very real to me when before it's not something I would ever take seriously because I had no need to.

So it took me quite a while to get over it...after I sent off a snippy email to you saying, "Why the hell didn't you tell me what the movie was about!"

Megan: I didn't make the connection.

Meredith: Well you wouldn't because that's not your frame of reference.

I think it really is one of the big issues still for me.

You have a child and your whole per-spective changes. Every movie where there is scary stuff going on they always put a child in harm's way to get the emotional reaction.

As soon as you have a child those scenes really kick you in the guts in a way they didn't before. It's really manipulative and formulaic and that's why they do it.

Lion King didn't upset me as much mind you, probably because it was the father, not the mother who dies. I certainly reacted emotionally to that, but no more than I would have before.

It's very directly the mother thing, and the father raising the sole son...

Megan: The very sweet sole son.

Meredith: That's right.

Courage looks you straight in the eye...
Courage is not afraid to weep,
and she is not afraid to pray,
even when she is not sure who
she is praying to.
When she walks it is clear
she has made the journey
from loneliness to solitude.
The people who told me she was stern
were not lying: they just forgot to mention
she was kind.

J. RUTH GENDLER

Megan's Journal

Day Zero - June 27, 2003

We arrived in San Francisco today for the big walk.
I have spent the week playing and sharing how incredible Northern California is with Meredith. We are
having so much fun, the walk has seemed almost
secondary.

But now that we are at the official hotel, it seems so
real. I'm just a little bit nervous. I'm uncomfortable
being around so many people. And I'm uncomfortable
being a "survivor" publicly. I am so glad Meredith is
walking with me.

We stood in about three lines to get all of our check-in procedure done. My big project for the day was to find a way to get Mom checked in for the walk. She's stuck in London on her way home from Italy. Some problem with the plane. We played a bit of overseas phone tag all day.

I'm really excited that I was able to raise enough donations for Mom to be able to walk. And it really doesn't seem right if she were to miss it.

I actually got to the Field Operations Director who was fantastic. He listened to me and immediately went to work on how to make it possible for Mom to join the walk whenever she was able to. We left the registration area with Mom's goodie bag and tent assignment in hand!

The last line we stood in was for merchandise. I was a bit overwhelmed and not prepared to buy anything - especially anything with a survivor label. Meredith bought both of us a hat. It was perfect. I would not have bought it on my own, and I realized that thankfully I would not have to wear it on my own.

After all the logistics were handled, we immediately went back to tourist mode. It was a fun and powerful night. We went to the opening of Charlie's Angels - the perfect movie to get us all fired up. Then we played video games to get out all of our aggressions. Then an amazing crab dinner and dancing in the Castro until midnight to celebrate Gay Pride weekend.

It was a great evening, although we did pay the price when the alarm went off at 4:30 a.m. the next morning!

Day One - June 28, 2003

I didn't sleep particularly well. I was excited and nervous both. It was dark and cold and foggy and damp at 5:30 a.m.. A standard summer morning in San Francisco.

The bus ride was quite the experience. Some people had signs and shirts they'd made in honor of or in memory of people they knew. One young woman had lost her Mom. I was really touched by her courage and her huge smile. And I didn't really want to think about people actually dying.

We waited for an hour for the opening ceremony to start. I had turned in my jacket and refused to admit that I was actually cold in my tank top. I pretended to be a tough triathlete, but it was obvious I was just stubborn.

The opening ceremony was moving, but thankfully they did not trigger a river of tears out of all of us. There was great music and a lot of excitement. I really felt a sense of anticipation - like something big was about to happen.

We wound our way through the fog, uphill to the Golden Gate Bridge. It was quite an unnerving experience to walk across the bridge without being able to see the towers above or the water below. Fortunately there was sun as soon as we hit the north side of the bridge.

From talking to people I knew who had done the walk in the past, I expected a lot more cheering and support and camaraderie on the walk than we actually experienced. We had a great time since we were all together, but we ran into some rather unpleasant people along the way. It's sad that those experiences seen to override the many amazing volunteers and support people who made the walk such a great experience.

As we came down into Sausalito, there were signs telling us to walk single file due to the narrow sidewalks. It wasn't much fun doing that for long periods of time, so we continued to walk side by side. A woman came past us really fast and said something like, "Can't you read the signs? You are supposed to walk single file!"

I was having a lot of fun and I was feeling pretty brave since I had talked myself into wearing my Survivor hat. I somehow missed the nasty tone in her voice and assumed she was a supporter. I said, "We were never very good at following rules." She actually said, "Well that's why you got it."

I was completely dumbfounded. Really frozen in my tracks. She was long gone with her horrible attitude before what she said really sunk in for me. That interaction stayed with me for some time. I don't understand where she was coming from that she could say such a thing. I should have chased after her and asked for a donation.

There was a party atmosphere as we hit each rest stop every two to three miles. The chant at the halfway mark was, "Drink, pee, eat and sunscreen."

Sharon stayed with us through mile 16 1/2 then took the bus back to camp and promised to have things ready for us when we got there.

Meredith and I started power-walking for we knew our next scheduled stop (completely un-sanctioned and un-official) was a bar at approximately mile 20.

We panicked slightly when the return route took a detour. Thankfully we did find a bar. Meredith hesitated since it really was a dive. I did not hesitate for a minute because I knew this was our one shot for a cold beer along the route.

We snuck in and out so fellow walkers wouldn't see us. We had a cover story in case we got caught - that we stopped in to wash our hands. There was someone shooting pool who made a nasty comment about breast cancer loud enough for us to hear. The woman with him gave him a good pop and the bartender came over to nicely chat with us. It was by far the best rest stop of the day!

As we came out of the bar, we started walking pretty fast again thanks to our rest stop. The first woman we caught up with was walking alone. She asked if she could walk with us for a while. I can't imagine doing that walk alone. She had flown out from the east coast to do it.

I was so excited to finally be spending time with Meredith after months of emailing that I was not totally thrilled about having to share. But I couldn't let her walk alone when she was looking for company. She went off on her own again at the next rest stop.

The walk was a real treat in that it provided hours and hours to talk about whatever came up. Unfortunately, there was a point when I was too tired to talk much at all.

There were different points at which we each thought we could not possibly keep up with the other. But we are both so stubborn we didn't breathe a word. We just kept walking - pain and all.

We chugged along, back over the bridge, knowing we were in the home stretch. It was cold as we hit fog again, but we kept going with renewed energy. We passed a lot of walkers at that stage. There was one woman who was falling behind her group. One of the fast walkers turned and gave her a thumbs up - I guess to ask if she was OK. What could the poor woman do but give a thumbs up back.

We were pretty horrified that people would dump their friends because they weren't walking fast enough. It was not a race and there was no prize for finishing first. At least that was our philosophy.

Somehow the course was incorrectly measured, and our walk kept going and going and going - long after we first spotted camp in Chrissy Field. The rumor around camp was that the actual walk the first day was closer to 30 miles than the scheduled 26.

I was cold and cranky and tired and really sore over the last hour. I just wanted to stop moving.

Since Mom was stranded in London, we had three of us camping and two tents. I'd been thinking about the best way to handle that all day. There was no way we could have any one of us sleeping alone, so we made the only logical decision - we all crammed into one tent and had a slumber party.

We talked for an hour, recapping our adventures from the day and laughed so hard it hurt. (Which isn't saying too much since everything hurt anyway). While other walkers stayed up dancing to the live music, we were passed out at 9 p.m., victims of our partying the previous night.

I felt such a sense of accomplishment and joy, and I slept well despite the cold, lumpy ground and inter-mittent fog horn.

Day Two - June 29, 2003

Day Two was painful. Meredith and I spent the morning in the medical tent getting our blisters wrapped. We stretched and packed our tent and gear and headed out. Uphill and foggy once again.

Mom flew in Saturday night, and met us in San Francisco with a friend at 7:00 a.m. Sunday. I really wanted Mom there and I knew it was a lot to ask her to ignore her jetlag to come and walk.

The 5 of us made a great team, and the 13 miles went pretty quickly. Although, for some reason, the route seemed to travel up and down every hill in San Francisco!

The highlight of the day were the bicycle police from San Jose. They would race up hills and then park and greet people. They seemed to be everywhere and were having a fabulous time. Their energy really made the struggle of walking bearable. They got a huge standing ovation as the rode into the finish area.

The closing ceremonies were incredibly moving. We all had pink T-shirts and honored everyone who participated in the walk. I felt so touched to have the most important people in my life there with me for the experience. It was almost exactly one year after my surgery. I was so aware of all I'd been through - physically and emotionally. And that I was one of millions to have gone through that experience.

Two important local organizations received checks that day as a result of the money raised by the walk, including a new program in San Francisco providing breast cancer screening to homeless women in the Tenderloin and a program in Marin to assist women with breast cancer living in rural communities.

Not wanting to end the day on the "pink" note and not wanting to stay on the brink of tears any longer than necessary, we had arranged for an antidote. We had a black Jaguar limousine pick us up at the finish. It was a great way to celebrate a fantastic weekend.

Breast Cancer as Identity

What lies behind us and what lies before us are
tiny matters
compared to what lies within us.

RALPH WALDO EMERSON

From: Meredith
Sent: Sunday, August 10, 2003

In all the discussions we've had and in the thinking
I've done about the first Avon Walk, the major significance for me is that it was the first time I really
began to acknowledge and incorporate my experience
of breast cancer into my identity. Not just the fact
that I was a survivor, but that the experience had
changed who I was as a person. And at the time,
I was really not happy with the changes I seemed to
be experiencing - particularly the emotional volatility.

My thoughts in leading up to doing the walk the first
time had been part of that whole, "It's over and done
with now, I'm back to normal and life will be back to
normal.", thing. My aim was to get through treatment
and then go do this incredible marathon walk that
would prove I was as strong and fit as ever and the
whole thing would be over and done with - I'd be
"fixed".

So by the time I eventually did the walk, the emotional
volatility was really starting to come to the fore,
along with the realisation that I wasn't the same

person as I used to be. And on that walk itself it was a huge conscious decision to decide to identify myself as a survivor - I didn't tell people that was why I was walking - I'd come there to research the event as a professional fundraiser! I still remember the effort and conscious will it took to decide to wear my survivor shirt the first night in camp, and to go buy a survivor cap and then to actually wear the damn thing the next day.

And the next two days were a pretty amazing experience of identifying with and being identified by other young women who were survivors and sharing experiences, which I hadn't done before because I wasn't keen on any of the support groups over here. So by the end of that walk I'd come to accept the "survivor" bit as part of who I am, and not necessarily try to reject or ignore it - that it didn't define who I was as a person, but was now part of me.

That whole walk was really a pretty heavy-duty processing and emotional roller coaster kind of journey for me.

So in the year since that walk and before this one I've obviously had another 12 months or more to work through all the impacts of this thing on my life. And the opportunity to talk through things and work them out in depth by email with you, which led me to being in a different head space entirely on the walk this time around.

The things that I said were different about this one are true in a macro sense - the people were certainly different along the walk and it was different to be doing it with you because of your own experiences and all we had shared by email.

My reflection now is that although there were some emotional moments on the walk and at the opening ceremony and closing ceremony, the biggest difference for me is that my own emotional state was of really being at peace and content with who I am and why I was there.

At the closing ceremony I had a sense of achievement at finishing the damn thing this time (although in total the distance was probably shorter than I walked last year!), particularly since my feet were an absolute mess. Feeling pretty damn stoked that not only had we finished the distance, but we had most definitely done it "our way" - partying till all hours the night before, sneaking off for beers en route, sneaking "refreshments" into camp.

I was definitely thinking about what was going on for you and in your head at the time - you know in another of life's other great non-coincidences, by my reckoning the walk must have been about 8 months after you finished chemo? The same time it was for me between chemo and my first Avon walk. I'm thinking you had your head together much better than me for that period of recovery.

And above all of that, although there were moments in the closing ceremony that I found moving, and emotional and inspirational, my main memory is of standing there with a feeling of peace and contentment about it all.

It really reflected that quote from Walt Whitman, "Strong and content, I travel the open road..."

I think that the realization that has come to me is that I have reached a point where I not only accept and incorporate the fact that I am a survivor as part of, but not the defining, piece of my identity, but I have also reached the point of accepting that I am a different person in many ways - emotionally, in my sense of priorities and what is important to me.

I don't think I'm a better or worse person than I was before, just different. Not good, not bad, just is.

And I think I am finally also past that feeling that this is something "wrong" that I have to "fix" so I'm back to "normal".

I don't need fixing, I am who I am now, and the journey from now on is continuing to find out who that is - and that's the next adventure.

From: Megan
Sent: Monday, August 11, 2003

One of the things I really love about our emails is that what you write triggers things in me. They allow me to make connections and put pieces together and to understand myself so much better. I haven't been thinking much about the significance of the walk, honestly. So, I am grateful for the thoughts that are coming to me as a result of your musings.

I have felt a bit of guilt over that fact that the event did not have more emotional significance for me. There have been other pieces of my journey that have been significantly more powerful. I think that really must be a result of where I happened to be in that overall journey.

When you talked about the Florida Walk being your big, challenging project to prove you and your life were back to normal, it immediately brought up our trip to Australia. That was the equivalent event for me. I was determined that a month in Australia, away from everyone and everything that had been relating to me as "sick", would be all the transition I needed back into my normal life.

The need to be bigger than life, to be super human, to have no limitations at all was incredibly strong. Not only were we traveling internationally for a month, weeks after I finished chemo, but I had to compete. Not only did I want to participate in the sailing, but I was determined to be as competitive as humanly possible. Even that wasn't enough. I had to do the triathlon. I HAD to do it. THAT was my identity. Breast cancer was in no way part of my identity. I had it. I dealt with it. It was over and done with.

Can you believe I did not once take a nap on that trip? I acted just like a normal person. Hung out at the yacht club and walked to the bus stop and squeezed in sightseeing on our minimal off time. I must have been so delirious.

Other than our conversation when we met, I did not talk about, think about or process anything related to breast cancer. You were the first person I'd ever met who was OK laughing about the experience. Complaining about the misery of it and coming up with cool ways to cope (like Tomb Raider and motorcycles).

And you were right there in January when I had my emotional meltdown. The triggers for me seemed to be hurting my knee and not being able to run, and the appearance of my suspicious lump. I had to finally face the fact that breast cancer had affected me in ways I did not yet understand and that the impact would be with me forever. I still don't want to believe that it changed me. But I cannot pretend to be the same as I was before.

The big pieces that came out of my months of depression that followed seem to be (and I doubt this list is all inclusive):

* Breast Cancer is part of my identity. It has helped shape and define who I am. And, it is not my whole identity. It is one little piece that works along with 20 other pieces.

* To quote my incredibly wise and insightful guide, "It's OK not to cope."

* Life is a great big unknown. There is not much you can do to prepare or protect yourself from what might come up.

* Living life to the fullest means enjoying each minute, whatever that looks like. Not necessarily being superwoman and doing everything in every moment.

So, the Avon Walk. I think I was really comfortable with me on that walk. I was OK with breast cancer as part of my identity. I did not need to cry over it anymore. I was overwhelmed at how many people were there participating. At how much effort had gone into producing the event. At how pervasive this disease is. I was also aware of the four people that different donors had lost to the disease. That made my part really seem not so hard. That to be there was such a gift.

The walk fit into our two weeks of adventures perfectly. It was not bigger or smaller than anything else we did. It was all an incredible celebration of life. I was really, really proud of having raised as much money as we did. And so grateful that Mom would come up to San Francisco at the crack of dawn the day after flying in from Europe.

And I was completely overwhelmed that you were there to share it with me. When you said you'd come over and do it, after talking with us for half an hour in Sydney, I was so excited. When you registered for the thing before I did, I was shocked. Having you actually there was so incredible. Powerful and exciting and wonderful.

It was just damn fun. Exactly the way it was supposed to be. We raised money for a great cause, we did something really challenging, we had a total blast doing it. There wasn't anything to process. It was just fun. Just life. Lots of love really. When you get to the core of anything in life, there is nothing but a lot of love. That is what I experienced on the walk. Tremendous love and joy.

Part IV:

Epilogue

Friendship and Connection

It's the friends that you can call up at 4 a.m. that matter.

MARLENE DIETRICH

When Meredith and I first met at the Yacht Club in Sydney, I knew it was something special, but I really had no idea how or why she was so important to me. I just knew this was someone I wanted to get to know, and that she represented living life fully after breast cancer.

We started emailing casually right after I returned home from Australia in November of 2002. Our email took a different turn when I discovered my first "suspicious lump" and had an emotional meltdown in January of 2003.

It was a breakthrough for me when I first called Meredith. I was in the middle of my upset in a hotel in Seattle. I was sure her husband John thought I was a lunatic. The breakthrough was that the call wasn't that expensive, the time difference was manageable, and that we could carry on a live conversation.

A few weeks later, we had another breakthrough. We spent three hours on the phone talking about anything and everything. I am so not a telephone person, and I couldn't believe we'd sustained a conversation for that long. And it was so much fun.

We soon after instituted weekly phone calls so we could keep up with each other live, along with our emailing.

When it was time for Meredith to come over for the Avon Walk in June, 2003, I was both excited and nervous. This was the one person with whom I had shared all of my fears and upsets around breast cancer. She knew when I was upset or excited by the tone of my emails alone.

We felt like good friends, but we'd never had more than a half hour conversation with each other in person. Would we have enough to talk about to fill a two week trip? Would we even like being around each other? Specifically, would she still like me once she'd been to my home and spent time with me?

Driving to the airport, I was so scared. It sounds silly looking back on all the emails and phone calls. How could I have been worried about having enough to talk about?

Thankfully, we got on beautifully. We did nonstop sightseeing for two weeks, completed the Avon Walk, celebrated at Disneyland and found we had even more in common than we thought.

And, we had breakthrough conversations around breast cancer. They were really hard at first. It was so much easier to communicate the hard stuff in an email. And we never talked about our upsets on the phone. Those conversations were reserved for fun stuff.

What we learned about each other is how strong we each are, and how we often use that strength to hide our fear and vulnerability. We found that it was safe to share a hint of that fear and vulnerability with each other. That it was OK to admit what we were really feeling underneath all our bravado. That we would be there for each other no matter what happened in our lives.

It was hard when Meredith left. Our friendship had leapt into a whole new realm, and I really missed not having her here. So often I would think how nice it would be to drop in on her and have a drink and just chat. I went so far as to calculate how much time and money it would take. If she'd lived anywhere in the U.S., I would have made it happen, but drop-ins just don't work between California and Australia.

Writing this book has forced us to look at areas of our breast cancer experience that we would likely have avoided otherwise. Knowing we were on this journey together made all the difference. I don't have to have all the answers. It is safe for me to look at what I am feeling and experiencing, and I know Meredith is there to listen and support and to call me on my B.S. when I'm glossing over or avoiding something. Just like I am there for her in the same way.

Meredith's second trip to the U.S. in October, 2003, was more relaxed. We were just excited to see each other and had none of the fear of actually being together. Our difficult conversations started in the cab from airport as soon as she landed. Some things are better said in person, and we'd been saving up for three months.

We found ourselves able to talk about anything and we never ran out of topics. When she left, our friendship was even stronger and more meaningful.

I still miss her when we aren't together, which is most of the time. And I am so grateful for email and inexpensive international calling cards! Our ability to move forward with this project and to impact the world came directly out of our friendship. I could never do this on my own.

I had a dream recently that I got sick again. I've never had a dream like that before. It was detailed and long and miserable. Meredith was there with me. And I knew I'd be OK.

I'd like to think that neither of us will ever face breast cancer again, or any other tragedy for that matter. And the truth is I don't know what we will face in our many years of life left to live. I do know that we'll always be there for each other and that life is so much richer and easier to face with a friend.

Megan Dwyer, December, 2003

New Beginnings

In the depths of winter, I finally learned that within me there lay an invincible summer.

ALBERT CAMUS

Writing this book has been an incredible experience. Often it seemed as though it would never be finished. Not because we couldn't find the topics to write about, but because our journey, like life, continues.

New challenges constantly arise that should be shared, but the time has come to draw a line on this book, and save our thoughts for the next edition.

One of those major challenges arose for me as we finished the book. After almost 9 years together, Sharon and I have separated.

It is still too soon and too raw for me to write about, and it will take time to find perspective on it all.

There is no doubt that breast cancer had a huge impact on our relationship, and the most difficult times we faced as a couple were through chemo and the months of recovery that followed.

I don't believe breast cancer was the cause of our breakup. The problems in our relationship were there before I was diagnosed. However, the added stress of my illness brought to the surface and magnified issues that had been there all along. Our relationship was always volatile, and breast cancer intensified things to a point where we could not continue as we were.

Breast cancer also challenged me personally to think hard about what I needed and wanted in my life, and to have the faith and courage to pursue it. Writing this book helped me to gain much needed clarity and to begin to make the choices I needed to move forward on my journey.

I don't know what the future holds for me now. Even with all the uncertainty and pain of dismantling my life, I feel strangely at peace, eager to discover whatever is next for me.

Travel has always been an important part of my life. I see it as time to reflect on the changes in my life, to grow more comfortable with the person I have become, and to discover my future path.

In August, I will be joining Meredith in Athens for the Olympic Games to see her friend Kristen represent Australia in yachting, 4 years to the day of her diagnosis.

In the birthplace of the Amazon legend, we will talk, and laugh, and cry, and sit on the beach, and drink champagne, and live every day to the fullest.

We hope that sharing our stories has helped you in your journey to find your strength and courage within.

Megan Dwyer, April, 2004

Make a pilgrimage. Go to ancient places.
Go wherever there are contemporary seekers.
Go in whatever way it works out. Just go.

JENNIFER LASH

About the Authors

Meredith Campbell

Meredith Campbell was a 33 year-old champion sailor, internationally recognized charity marketing professional and mother of one when diagnosed with breast cancer in 2000.

Meredith lives in Australia with her husband of 17 years, John and their son, Dexter.

Megan Dwyer

In June 2002, just weeks after launching a new career as a real estate agent, Megan Dwyer was diagnosed with breast cancer at the age of 35.

Prior to her diagnosis Megan had combined successful careers in structural engineering, marketing, business and life coaching with amateur competition in water polo, triathlons and marathon running.

Amazon Heart

Communication - Community - Celebration

One person can have a profound effect on another.
And two people...well, two people can work miracles.
They can change a whole town.
They can change the world.

DIANE FROLOV and ANDREW SCHNEIDER

"Amazon Heart - Coping with Breast Cancer Warrior Princess Style" is one part of a much larger and ambitious project to meet the needs of women living with breast cancer.

Amazon Heart is a series ground breaking initiatives founded by and for women living with breast cancer.

In addition to our book, we are developing a world first email based one to one peer support program for women living with breast cancer.

We are also launching a series of events to develop peer support networks, community and media awareness of the concerns and needs of women living with breast cancer. Most importantly, the events are about coming together, celebrating life fully and having a fantastic time!

Events in the pipeline include a motorcycle adventure down the coast of California in October 2004, with future plans for surfing safaris and trekking adventures.

Check out our website at www.amazon-heart.com and sign up for Amazon Drum our email newsletter to stay up to date with our latest plans!

Join the Tribe!

Share the Amazon Spirit with Your Friends and Family
Order Now

☐ YES, I want _____ copies of Amazon Heart - Coping with Breast Cancer Warrior Princess Style for $14.95 each.

☐ YES, I am interested in having Megan Dwyer or Meredith Campbell speak or give a seminar to my company, association, school or organization. Please send me information.

Include $3.95 for shipping and handling for one book, and $1.95 for each additional book. California residents must include 8-1/4% sales tax.

Payment must accompany orders. Allow 3 weeks for delivery. U.S. orders only.

My check or money order for $ _____ is enclosed.
(Make payable to Artemisia Enterprises, LLC)
Please charge my ☐ Visa   ☐ Mastercard   ☐ American Express

Name_____

Organization _____

Address _____

City/State/Zip_____

Phone_____ email_____

Card #_____

Exp. Date_____ Signature_____

ORDER ONLINE AT WWW.AMAZON-HEART.COM
or
Send payment to:
Artemisia Enterprises, LLC
P.O. Box 59233
San Jose, California 95159
Fax: 978-268-8644